Phantoms Fill the
Southern Skies

Jeff Lawhead

ISBN 978-1-9393061-4-2

First Edition

Printed in the United States of America
Published by 23 House Publishing
SAN 299-8084
www.23house.com

Note: The name of this book comes from a report of an extreme and prolonged supernatural disturbance that took place in several areas of California between 1989 and 1990. A woman named Jackie Hernandez and a photographer named Jeff Wheatcraft were being stalked by an unusually aggressive entity and one night they tried to communicate with it using Ouija board.

They asked the entity several questions; including "How many ghosts reside among the living?" its answer was "Phantoms fill the skies around you."

Dedicated to Ge'ne Kea-Lawhead,
who took my interest in the worlds of the dead
and made them come to life.

Contents

Introduction

The cultures of the American South are as rich as the soil beneath our feet – the same soil that made this corner of the United States so attractive to the many settlers and wealthy landowners who built their farms in the Appalachian Mountains and the broad spans of flat land in the valleys and plains beyond. The South is a major cradle of civilization for the history of the United States, starting with the explorations of the early Paleo-Indians to the Five Civilized Tribes of Native Americans that descended from them many thousands of years later. This history continued on with the Spanish and French settlements of the mid-16th century, the British colonization efforts that followed in the early 17th century, and the many other European families who were attracted to the prospects of a new world.

When we look back at the tapestry of our heritage in the South, we see threads of Cherokee, Chickasaw, Choctaw, Creek, Seminole, British, Scottish, French, Spanish, Irish, Germanand African American ancestry woven together with all their homeland customs, religious motivations, family traditions, hopes, beliefs and fears. You can see the remnants of them even today in museums of Appalachian culture, in the abandoned farmhouses that pocket the highlands, and the evolution of the Southern people that came from those natives and settlers. Maybe more so here than anywhere else in the country, in the South our history *is* our lifeblood.

But that history, as proud as it is, is also a very dark and disturbing one. Some of the most treacherous evils committed on U.S. soil have occurred here, and it becomes small wonder that stories of ghosts and spirits would permeate throughout our history as much as the facts themselves.

What do ghosts have to do with history? Well, although, you won't learn about ghosts in school, the answer to that question is "pretty much everything." Ghosts and ghost stories literally *are* history. If you see a ghost, you see the viscous form of someone who died anywhere from a few years ago to hundreds or thousands of years ago. If you research who they might be, you might be taken back to 1782 or 1854 to learn how they arrived there and what they did for that young community. You will learn about ancient diseases, lovers that never returned from war and people who met with foul play as a result of an impoverished life. The possibilities are endless, and something as a simple as a little campfire tale can teach us much of what we had to go through to get where we are today.

It stands to reason then that the folklore of supernatural activity is just as rich as the academic version of history. Phantoms *fill* the Southern skies – it seems that every square inch of land below the Mason-Dixon Line is haunted with innumerate varieties of ghosts, spirits, boogers, boogeymen, witches and demons. They come out on the darkest of nights and hide between the trees. They live in holes on the sides of cliffs, underneath the waters of the rivers, and spend their seemingly never-ending supply of days and nights sitting on their own headstones, waiting for you to come around.

Why are they here? What do they come for? Ghosts are as individualistic in death as they were in life, and each has a different story capitalized by a different motive. Throughout the history of the South, there was rarely a time when it wasn't

2

a large scale battlefield between race, states, ideas and even countries. It was a major front for the American Revolution and the Civil War, a bleeding ground between the invading whites and the Native American tribes, and a war zone for African American slaves who fought for freedom. Thousands upon thousands of their ghosts are said to remain, thinking that those battles are still going on.

And then there are some that say that evil spirits, those incorporeal beings who exist only to torment the living, are drawn here to feed off the darkness of these historical horrors. Stories of their dark presence throughout the South have existed since at least the days of the Cherokee, and continue to the present.

With so much history and so much folklore deriving from it, a complete volume of Southern ghost lore would be twice the size of the King James Bible. This book you are holding is only a small collection of some of my favorite finds in Tennessee, Georgia, Kentucky, Alabama and North and South Carolina, a mixture of obscure and very creepy reports alongside classic legends that no compilation on ghost lore should do without. I have even included my own paranormal experience that occurred in the Summer of 2011.

And on that note, I will close by saying this book is not intended to provide any scientific evidence for the case of supernatural. To date, no scientific research has ever produced anything confirming or debunking life after death (and I personally doubt science will ever confirm it either way). The concepts related to them remain open questions, but this is not a book about science; this book is about folklore and history. Even in our modern society, full of logic and advancement, these stories persist with a vengeance. History refuses to remain forgotten and no matter how far we go, we're always haunted by our past.

Thank you and enjoy!

What Are Ghosts?

Even as our society moves further and further away from things it considers "supernatural" (an arbitrary term as nature cannot be transcended, and therefore any ghostly presence or paranormal occurrence would, in fact, be a product of nature), there is an equally strong movement from believers and supporters into taking what has been gathered from the thousands of stories and reports of ghostly activity existing throughout the country and organizing it into a sub-science of its own.

The differences between a "ghost" and a "poltergeist," for example, are more substantial than one might first think. There are many different types of hauntings, but often books on the subject shy away from specifying or giving better insight into what they are, which would allow us to learn more about the history and nature of ghosts, spirits and the other entities that are said to roam in the darkness of the South.

In this brief section, I would like to do just that in the interest of putting a modern, updated perspective on a fascinating subject. You never know... you just might need this information yourself, should you ever come into contact with a ghost.

* * * * *

What is a **Ghost**? Isn't anything that comes back from the dead to haunt us a ghost? Well, often they all get lumped in together in the same category, but that does not make it accurate.

A ghost is probably the simplest, purest form of a spiritual presence that was once a living identity. Although it has no solid body and it has no physical properties, it might be able to do things as it once did when it was alive, which may include retaining a recognizable shape based on what it looked like just before it died, using a recognizable voice (though sometimes not its own), moving simple objects like papers, keys, glasses and so forth, communicating messages either clearly or cryptically, and moving through walls and floors while ironically being "chained" to the location it is haunting.

Ghosts have been at the back of society's mind since ancient times, and reports of them are as old as death itself. Spirits were a big part of the culture of ancient Egypt, the religions of Mesopotamia, and the classic era of Greece, among others. Every single country in the world has stories of ghosts and paranormal activity, and their cultural response naturally varies alongside it. It seems to be commonly agreed throughout these cultures that a ghost is simply the remaining consciousness of an individual that did not pass on to an afterlife or reincarnate back onto the Earth. The body died, but the individual did not.

Ghosts are typically described as being unable to pass on to the next stage of existence because of an attachment to something on Earth. They may not be able to reconcile with the fact that they have died, or even recognize that they are dead, and use that to justify remaining with a location, item or even person they were attached to in life. Many ghosts are described as neutral, meaning no harm whatsoever to the living. Seeing a ghost might be frightening only because we were not expecting to see it, and because it goes against what we used to believe was the most unshakable fact of life: "when you die, *you don't come back.*"

Some ghosts are even described as being positive, beneficial entities that help out around the house, or warn of something to come in the near future. Forewarning spirits may also take the form of a "twin" called a **Doppelganger** to act as an omen for the person who might see someone that looks exactly like them in a distant crowd. Stories of doppelgangers are quite rare, but they exist even in Tennessee (see *Mysteries of the South*).

Then there are ghosts who are described as being unbearably dark and negative – commonly referred to as **Evil Spirits**. These are ghosts that have, for whatever reason, decided to impress their sorrow and hatred back to the living with a variety of atmospheric hostility. They seem to retain a stronger attachment to their Earthly passions and possessions more than a common ghost, and therefore may take more aggressive action in keeping things the way they want they. Others are victims of crimes or other wrongdoings that refuse to accept their circumstances, and feel the need to take it out on anyone who crosses their invisible boundaries. They do not grow or learn, they simply stagnate in their hatred and usually cannot be moved without an exorcism or blessing.

An evil spirit may not be anything more than an unusually uncomfortable feeling in a concentrated area. A feeling of bitter cold or nausea in the laundry room of the house, for example, may indicate the presence of an evil spirit. There are feelings of "being watched," unsettling voices may be heard, touching or even breaking objects with an evil spirit haunting the area. Activity of an evil spirit may be range from mild behavior to outright horrific and thoroughly dangerous, as ancient and modern ghost lore illustrate.

Poltergeists are also well-known for physical disturbances and often they blur the line between evil spirits and other phenomena, but the main difference is that a poltergeist may not be derived from a once-living individual. A poltergeist may be a different manifestation or force entirely. Some stories and researchers suggest a poltergeist may not be an entity at all, but an unconscious psychic movement of a living person under stress or experiencing a burst of energy.

A poltergeist may be more destructive than an evil spirit, but its activity is far more random and chaotic as opposed to being attached to certain objects and boundaries. Unlike a traditional haunting, a poltergeist may show up at any time, leave at any time and only stay for a few months at the maximum (although some cases have lasted more than a year), as opposed to a haunting which may last for hundreds of years or more.

Finally, the last major category of entities that haunt people and places is a malicious combination of all of the above. Stories of **Demons** reigning over graveyards, abandoned houses and other strange places are surprisingly abundant in folklore, especially in the South.

Unlike ghosts and evil spirits, demons are not previously living people; they are highly functional, somewhat intelligent, and often invisible forces that prey on mortal life in any way they see fit. Demons have few limits, may take on an infinite number of forms if they choose to have one, and are not necessarily bound to any place or item. If they choose a person to torment, they may follow that person around indefinitely. Objects may be moved or broken in a scheme designed to provoke its prey or create obstacles if a person tries to remove its presence from the area. It may manipulate nature or create complex forms of mischief with or without a clear message trying to be conveyed. It may even get violent, pushing a person down the stairs, leaving claw marks or similar slashes across their bodies, choking a person with invisible force, or even try to kill. Deaths by paranormal means are very, very rare (naturally, as no respected medical authority would allow a supernatural cause to be published on a death certificate), but even in Tennessee, it's been said that John Bell of the famous Bell Witch legend is the only man to have ever been killed by a demon, which is what many believe the Bell Witch might have been (see *Witches of the Hollars*).

The most frightening reports of demon activity involve possession. Although these stories are also rare and sometimes met with skepticism even by supporters of paranormal activity, there have been some very famous stories and incredible reports of demonic possession throughout world history, including the Loudun and Louviers possessions in France during the mid-17th century which featured public exorcisms with over seven-thousand people in attendance, the possession of Anneliese Michel, which inspired *three* movies since 2005, and the exorcism of Roland Doe which inspired *The Exorcist*. Even Jesus of Nazareth was said to have met people who were under their influence in the New Testament and was successful in driving out the demonic hosts.

Interestingly enough, while conventional Christianity, particularly as it is practiced here in the South, is very quick to dismiss most or all of these categories of paranormal activity, invoking the name and power of Christ is often the only exercise that will exorcise these entities out and restore order to the area. Sometimes only a simple blessing of the house will do it, other times a designated exorcist or demonologist will be called to talk to the entity and convince or force them to leave. Whether it's the strength of religious faith in the South or the strength of the power of suggestion, something in these rituals genuinely seems to work in returning wayward spirits and forces back to the realms they belong in (something I can personally attest to much later in the book).

* * * * *

There are many, many other forms the dreaded unknown will take in folklore throughout the South and beyond, but as it applies here in Tennessee, Georgia, Kentucky, Alabama and the Carolinas, most reports of paranormal entities fall under these major categories. They may appear in full-torso forms or tiny orbs of light that resemble nothing else in nature. They may haunt or be exposed only under certain conditions and some activity may even be residual, where the individual has passed on to the next life and some of their life force remained behind, repeating the same actions over and over again in an existential loop.

The possibilities are truly endless, and the sheer volume of ghost lore here in the South reflects that. With so many fascinating living things native to Dixie, is it any wonder they would get even more fascinating in death? No matter how heavy the darkness is, the mystery of what we could find inside is alluring even beyond all logic and reason.

Now that we know what we're looking for, let's begin our journey into the darkness...

Ghosts in the Graveyard

There is nothing pleasant about a cemetery. Even with bright flowers, sunshine and images of angels adorning headstones and tombs, it doesn't completely take away that fundamental fear of death that all humans carry with them until they die. Passing by a graveyard reminds us that, someday, all that we have known will no longer be with us. We remember when we put our loved ones there, in boxes heavily decorated for no one to see, all dressed up with nowhere to go, to spend years and years trapped in the cold ground, and we struggle with the ideas that our elders, brothers, and children will all eventually be buried there too. To someone who has not found peace with this fate, a cemetery may be the scariest thing on Earth.

And yet, with this knowledge of the human condition in mind, something interesting happens to the lucky few who get a very good glimpse into the afterlife when they see the glowing form of a man standing over his own burial plot – they get *scared*. One might think it would be cause for celebration – you now know for a very good fact that death is not the end, the greatest fear throughout the history of mankind, and it *terrified* you? How does that work?

The answer may be fairly simple – mankind has always been afraid of the unknown and death is the greatest unknown of all. As I mentioned earlier, we live with the knowledge that "once you die, you don't come back," and we designated this as a fact simply because we can't do any better. Now the unknown is literally walking around against the facts of life and watching us as we run away. The body makes this realization much faster than our brains can with the fear factor not far behind it. Logic comes in at a very distant third.

With the grave as the gateway to the great unknown, it does not take long before people encounter mysteries surrounding them in the cemeteries, and the South is home to a morbidly large quantity of them in cemeteries great and small. Family cemeteries are especially numerous here in the South as farms needed large families to do the work with dangerous tools, unbearable conditions, and no reasonable medical help nearby if someone was ill or injured. Stories of deceased fathers and grandfathers coming back to check on the old farm abound throughout the Southern states. Some spirits even bring a good sense of comfort to the families that encounter them, knowing that their loving presence is still with them and will remain so forever.

And then there are stories of cemetery haunts you *better* be afraid of. These ghosts and spirits are not just going against what we used to believe about nature, they are menacing, freak creatures that should not be taken lightly, whether you believe in them or not.

Some genuinely strange entities conquer the graves of the South, and you may want to pay attention to some of the ones listed here, you won't want to be out in *these* cemeteries after dark!

* * * * *

The first stop is the aptly named **Hell's Church** of Canton, Georgia, located in Cherokee County. Canton is a fairly old city, having been the site of the second significant gold rush in

U.S. history with the 1829 Georgia Gold Rush, a heartland for the Cherokee Nation until 1838 when federal troops started moving them west as part of the "Trail of Tears," and a major source of denim goods in the country with the Canton Cotton Mills until it closed in 1979.

And while the history of Canton is fairly conventional, the history of its famous church is not. Today, the building looks like any other modern, modest-sized worship center for the locals to congregate with a pavilion for dinners and picnics in the back, a pathway through the woods, and a rather large-sized cemetery (appropriate for a Southern church with roots going back to the 19th century) across the street, but it's a far cry from what it used to look like. No one is quite sure when it was first constituted, but the consensus seems to be somewhere around 1886 when it was first built as the New Hightower Baptist Church. The church started out as a log cabin that served as both a place of worship and a school until a proper structure was built a few years after that. It stood for over a hundred years until it was burned down in 1990.

But the story takes its first strange turn before that in the 1970s when the church became a hangout spot for underage teens to smoke, drink, party and do things delinquents typically do. Rumors got started that the church was haunted – it was reported that there was a figure moving around in the dark, lights illuminating in some of the rooms, eyes appearing in the windows, and even something banging against the old organ inside. It was later discovered that a homeless man was using the church at night and doing things to scare the kids away. His plan backfired, as he underestimated the curiosity of teenagers spreading ghost stories and sneaking out at night to see if they're true. While rumors continued, it seemed like any possible truth to the hauntings were laid to rest.

Then the story took another strange turn when a mutilated body was found on the church grounds in the 1980s. The rumors then twisted from simple hauntings to stories of devil worship and Satanic ritual abuse, similar to other accusations of devil worship that held the nation in the grip of paranoia later in that decade. Some stories went as far as to say there were deaths in the baptismal pool and more evil worship activity going on in the woods in the back. While it was true that a body was found, no evidence of satanic activity or devil worship (there is a difference between the two) was ever discovered.

The rumors continued unabated and finally escalated in 1990 when a group of teenagers burned down the church with homemade firebombs, believing they were fighting back at the devil worshippers. The leader of the group was a high school senior who believed he was punishing a man who murdered his father sixteen years prior. One story suggests this murderer might've been a member of the church's supposed secret cult, but no other connections have been made. The church burned to the ground and was rebuilt for its third incarnation in 1992, enjoying a healthy congregation and continuing to occasionally attract vandals well-versed in these legends.

But then the story takes a final and, by now, very unexpected twist in 2005 when a team from the Foundation of Paranormal Researchers set out to investigate the church, cemetery and surrounding areas to see how well the persistent rumors hold up... and *did* find potential evidence for a haunting. The team experienced very negative atmospheric impressions – some had chest pains as they approached the pavilion in the back, others experienced increased anxiety around the hanging tree and felt something was watching them from the woods in the back. Photos they took on the church grounds revealed orbs around the gravesites and hanging tree. Their final report, while inconclusive, suggested the activity may be coming from a secret Cherokee burial ground somewhere onsite or nearby. This means, for all the senseless accusations and abuse the building had suffered over the years, it was the *cemetery* responsible for all the reported activity onsite, not the church. If a more dramatic example of irony exists in Southern ghost lore, I've yet to see it.

Even today, though, the site is said to be haunted with the sound of faint piano music late at night and a tree that bleeds as a dark remnant from its days as a hanging spot.

With a back-story that complicated, it comes as no surprise Hell's Church remains a hotspot for ghostly gossip and the occasional vandal squatting in the moonlight, hoping to catch a glimpse of something otherworldly through the windows or just add another footnote of senseless destruction to the church history records. The church now employs security at night, but whether or not it will prevent yet another twist in the story sometime in the near future will remain to be seen...

* * * * *

A simpler story with a more pronounced history is the story of **Alice Flagg** from Murrells Inlet, South Carolina in Horry County, a seaside town near Georgetown County widely touted as the "seafood capital of South Carolina." It was once famous as a fishing town and known for its numerous Southern plantations, including the Wachesaw Plantation that was once owned by the Flagg family in the mid-19th century.

The Flaggs were a wealthy and traditional Southern dynasty led by Dr. Allard Flagg after the death of his father, the previous patriarch of the clan. He and his mother oversaw the affairs of the family as they all lived in their seaside family home, the Hermitage. Besides Allard were two other children, Dr. Arthur Flagg and Alice. Both doctors were courting two sisters of the Ward aristocrats from the neighboring Brookgreen Plantation. Alice herself became fast friends with the Ward sisters when they came over to the Hermitage during the courtship, but while she enjoyed the exquisite revelry they often had, her heart was set in more modest means with a man named John Braddock.

Braddock was not a rich man, nor was he any more renowned than any other turpentine dealer of the day. He was an honest, unpretentious, simple worker who met Alice while shopping one day in town. Later, he come to call on Alice at the Hermitage, but Dr. Allard, bewitched by the caste system of the wealthy, found the man to be wholly unsuitable for his sister and turned Braddock away from the property. When Alice learned of this, she confronted her brother and they had a major argument where he forbade her from having contact with anyone "beneath the notice of a Flagg."

But Alice was rebellious, and invited him back to the Hermitage a few weeks later to go for a ride in his horse-drawn carriage. Soon after this, Braddock gave her an engagement ring. At the same time, Dr. Allard was conspiring with his mother and brother to find ways to "civilize" Alice, and the minute he saw the ring Braddock had given her, Allard demanded Alice remove it and give it back to her simple beau with regrets. Alice agreed only temporarily, meaning to put a ribbon through it and continue to wear it without being seen.

Not long after that, Alice was sent to school in Charleston where she continued to pine for her betrothed. She did not enjoy the change of scenery and the distance from her lover was difficult to bear.

Then, one night, as she was attending a ball at the St. Cecilia Society, Alice fell ill with what came to be diagnosed as malarial fever. Dr. Allard was called and he came to Charleston to take Alice back to the Hermitage. She laid in bed, delirious, while he packed her things, and took her back on a difficult, jostling and jolting journey that made her illness even worse. It took four days to reach their home and Alice fell into a coma.

At some point, Dr. Allard found her engagement ring and flew into a silent rage. He blamed Braddock for his sister's illness – if it hadn't been for him, she would never have contracted the fever. He went outside and threw the ring into a nearby creek.

The next morning, Alice awoke and clutched for the ring that she held, on the ribbon, near her heart... but it wasn't there. Whatever she had left of her mind scrambled furiously and she clawed herself trying to find it. She called for it with what was left of her voice, but it did not return. Her reason for living was gone, and so she had nothing left to live for. She slipped back into a coma and soon died.

Today, Alice's story is one of the most famous ghost stories of South Carolina, as her presence is still seen and felt not only in the Hermitage, but at her gravesite as well at the All Saints Waccamaw Episcopal Church. She may be seen near her gravesite, clutching her chest and continuing to look for the ring she lost alongside her life more than one-hundred-and-sixty years ago. Some people say that if you walk backwards in a circle around her grave (between eight to thirteen times) and call her name twice, she will appear before you, still trying to find that ring.

She may even tug or pull yours off, if she's jealous of the one you're wearing...

* * * * *

Tales of love flourishing beyond the divide of mortality are very well-known in Southern ghost lore, and while Alice's story is truly heartbreaking, it is a much lighter example compared to one from Dyersburg, Tennessee, in Dyer County, where we travel to a cemetery that is said to be haunted by an unnerving figure called the **Darkman**.

17

Darkman is said to be the classic image of the "black aggie" legend – an intensely evil spirit, formerly of a witch or another diabolic figure, which moves around the graveyard as an indiscernible form, hidden from human notice until they see its bright eyes piercing the void and looking like they're coming out of nowhere. A black aggie is almost entirely negative and, with few exceptions, is not interested in anything other than frightening anyone who might be wandering around the mortuary grounds much later than they should be.

Darkman, however, is one of those exceptions.

The spirit is said to be that of a man who lived in a two-room shack near Dyersburg before the turn of the 19th century. Dyersburg experienced some major growth in the mid-to-late 1800s when it was a steamboat hub that grew into a river town, experienced an industrial boom in 1879 when it became an exporter of timber to markets in St. Louis, and the creation of a sawmill, timber mill, and planing mill not long after that. Presumably, this man was employed somewhere along those industries as he was making money in an area with just over two thousand people in it, among four new booming industries, and was stashing it away somewhere, but for some reason, he and his family lived in dire poverty.

The reason? According to legend, the man was an obsessive miser who cared more about his money than his family. He had a wife that was wasting away from neglect and children that had to be fed by neighbors so they didn't starve to death. The man was relatively well-known in the community; either by his connections or by his infamous hoarding, but no one seemed to know what he was so paranoid of that he had to hide his money even from his desperately underprivileged family. It could be that he wasn't afraid of anything and just simply had a truly evil heart pounding in his chest every time he thought about his beloved treasure trove filling someone else's hands.

Miraculously, the children survived and grew into adults that moved far away from the miser they called their father, but their mother, who had to resort to wearing rags, eating from the garbage and struggling every single day to keep them all alive, finally wore out and died soon after they left. The man was now old and hated by the community, and spent his last years as a recluse until he too wore out, alone with only his secret stash of money as the only love he had left.

When he died, his name was so tarnished that no one attended his funeral, not his children, not even a preacher would acknowledge his life on Earth. The only movement his death inspired to the community was an effort to find this scandalous secret stash in his small, two-room shack. The entire building was reduced to dust before the ironic scavengers gave up trying to find it (why they thought it was there would be an excellent question to ask them – if there was a large treasure trove in such a small hovel, wouldn't the wife have found it at some point and used it to feed and clothe her children?) and now nothing remains of the story today, except, of course, for the man himself.

For decades, his black shade has been reported to be seen haunting the Dyersburg cemetery, gliding over the headstones at night and acting in a strange way. His story grew and became a genuine town legend for generations of children growing up and venturing out to the graveyard to see if Darkman would rise, and many ran home screaming with their desires fulfilled beyond their wildest dreams.

It is said that, years later, one believer of Darkman did not run away and, instead, observed the spirit's activities in the graveyard. He found that the Darkman would act in a pattern and eventually settle in on one grave in particular – the grave of his former wife. When the black aggie came over the burial plot, it would kneel down and present a loaf of bread, out of nowhere, and lay it on the granite. The spectral loaf would sink into the ground, and Darkman would then disappear.

It became clear to the young observer that the Darkman wasn't simply the evil spirit of an evil man, it was a soul trapped in a perpetual state of contrition. Having denied his wife bread to put on the table in life, he must spend his afterlife making up for his heartless negligence. How long he is condemned to do this is anyone's guess, but as the story continues today, it seems he still has a long ways to go to make up for his miserly sins.

It is worth noting that the term "black aggie" has usually referred to a statue in the Druid Ridge Cemetery of Baltimore that was placed over the grave of General Felix Agnus in 1926. This statue gathered its own volume of urban legends with rumors it would come to life at night, flashing red eyes at those who were trespassing near it, that ghosts in the cemetery convened at the statue once every year, and that anyone who sat in its lap during the night would be broken and dead by morning. Other stories of haunted statues in local cemeteries might also refer to them as black aggies, and it seems like the term has been spread out over the years and been tacked onto any dark entity said to haunt a graveyard.

* * * * *

Love as a marital bond is one of the largest driving forces in ghostly legends that derive from the gravesite – after all, they only vowed to part at death... that didn't mean they wouldn't try to come back. Love is an inescapable force to which all things are subsequent. It is a force beyond logic and reason, and when that bond is shared, it creates an illumination that divides the darkness and leads us through the path of life, and when that bond is broken, the darkness may consume us and end that path without warning.

Such is the story of **The Cursed Tombstone** from Eastern Kentucky, as darkness consumed Southern man Carl Pruitt and turned him into an invisible and unstoppable killing machine.

In 1938, Carl came home after a long day at work completely unaware it was the last day of work he would ever have. He expected his wife to be cooking their dinner as she always did about the time he returned, but this evening, the kitchen was empty and she was nowhere to be found... or so he thought, until he opened the door to their bedroom and found her in bed with another man.

Carl was not able to exact his rage on the quick lothario that scrambled to the front door with his clothes falling behind him, but his wife had nowhere to go. Insane with a million questions running through his mind, Carl grabbed a chain lying nearby and strangled his wife to death. When he was able to see through his blinding fury, he saw what he had done to his once-lovely wife, and what that was going to mean for him. Carl committed suicide before dawn the next morning.

His wife's family was not able to sympathize with Carl's plight and they refused to forgive him for taking her away from them. He was buried in a different county where he could rot for his sins by himself.

But barely a week after Carl was buried, a series of circles started forming around his tombstone. In two months time, the circles formed what seemed to be a cross pattern of chains around his burial plot. Visitors to the cemetery started taking notice of his grave, and being superstitious mountain folk, it wasn't long before they started whispering rumors to one another about what could be going on there.

A month later, some local boys rode their bikes to the cemetery to see the tombstone they had been hearing about. One boy felt the need to throw a rock at the tombstone to prove how brave he was against curses and broke off a small piece of the edge. When they were riding back home, the boy who successfully chipped the tombstone suddenly lost control of his bike and slammed into a tree. The collision somehow snapped his sprocket chain and caused it to wrap around his neck with such voracity that he couldn't get it off. It choked him until he was dead.

Many thought the boy died of a freak accident, but not his mother. She was well aware of the tombstone's reputation and went to get revenge with an axe. She struck it several times but, reportedly, was not able to damage it (which seems strange considering how easy it was for her son to chip it with a rock) and left the cemetery with a weight of disappointment on her shoulders. The next day, she was found strangled to death too, by some bizarre altercation with the laundry clothesline in her backyard.

Now the neighbors were getting worried and one of them tried to take it into his own hands to stop the curse. He went to the graveyard with three members of his family, driving past it by horse and buggy, and proceeded to *shoot it* with his pistol (a very odd choice of weapon for a stationary stone monument). He managed to break off some more stone from the edges, but the discharge of the weapon scared the horses and they took off wildly down the road. They came to a sharp curve; the neighbor fell forward and was strangled by the trace chains of the buggy, becoming the third victim of the curse.

What in the world was going on here? The townspeople were now terrified and went so far as to pressure their congressman to do something about it. Likely rolling his eyes and groaning at the request, he at least sent two policemen to investigate and try to pacify their fears. Neither officer took the assignment seriously and mocked the curse as they took pictures and trod on the scene. When they left, one of the officers saw an orb of light following them from the cemetery in the rearview mirror. The driver lost control of the car and hit a chained link between two posts, throwing both out of the windshield. The passenger officer survived, but the driver got caught in the chain and was nearly decapitated.

The last death attributed to the tombstone came years after, as another emboldened citizen tried to break the curse by breaking the slab in the 1940s. He was also found strangled around a chain.

It seemed like Carl's writhing anger would never be satisfied. Even in death, he could not find the answer for why the love of his life betrayed him, and the darkness that festered with his twisted soul fed on his anguish until it needed more. What could stop this very literal of chain of disasters from continuing?

That answer came in 1958 when a strip mining company came to uproot the entire cemetery for their operation. The once-immortal monument finally fell in the demolition, and the curse was officially over. Oddly enough, no deaths were reported as a final vengeance from Carl Pruitt for this destruction. Could it be that there just wasn't a chain handy this time around?

* * * * *

Of course, not all stories of graveyard haunts involve tales of love separated or squandered; some just feature accounts of horrific beings that stomp the burial grounds when the nights are thick with black mists, in full moonlight, in or around the time of Samhain (Halloween). Tales like the **Red Ash Cemetery** in Caryville, Tennessee, feature demonic figures adorned with the classic characteristics of the devil (the red goat man with horns and a pentagram). Others whisper of Lucifer making more subtle monuments of evil incarnate, such as the church of the **Cemetery Mountain** woods in Munford, Alabama, where a book of Satanic rituals is said to rest on an old podium, and refuses to leave the premises as anyone who picks it up finds it will get heavier with each step they take away from it until it simply drops to the ground. The graveyard near to it is also said to be infested with imps, goblins and a black dog that will sometimes appear with its dead master.

If it is true that some souls are meant to be dragged to Hell upon death, then someone downstairs is doing a very poor job of closing the gates afterward. Surely every cemetery in the South, no matter how large, small, new or old it might be, is said to be visited by at least one demon on regular occasions. With Christianity being a major facet of Southern living, the fear of the devil and his minions still haunts many today, fear personified by the stories we hear and the stories we tell.

I remember hearing this story back when I was in middle school. There is a church in Atoka, Tennessee, at almost the western-most point of the state in Tipton County, called the **Bethel Assembly of God Church** or the Bethel Cumberland Presbyterian Church, depending on where you hear it. This church is apparently dated before the 1850s and before Atoka became an incorporated town in 1872, with the cemetery dating back just as early. The history for this particular church seems to be rather obscure, but still well-known for the demonic spirit that haunts it.

The version I heard back some eighteen years ago was that a thief from a much earlier era (perhaps between the 19th and early 20th century) got caught in a storm running from the police after they found his hiding spot. He broke into the church to find shelter and remain hidden, and spent the night in there only to be woken up in the darkness by a sound that was coming from a confessional in the corner of the room that he did not see before (this should've been the first clue that something was wrong – Presbyterian churches do not have confessionals).

Drawn to it, the thief went inside, knelt down and a voice asked him to confess his sins. One by one, the thief poured his heart out to the mysterious man on the other side, but as his sins went on and got darker by the minute, the man on the other side started laughing and mocking him. He said something to the effect of, "those are some heavy sins, my son... we'll have to send you to hell *now!*" and the thief ran for his life.

When he got back out in the storm, he was chased in the graveyard by a demon that had the head of a dog, the body of a lion, and red, evil eyes. The thief was almost caught by the demon when he leapt over the gate and then found he was all alone. This demon, evidently, could not pass through the gates of the cemetery as its job is to guard the area at night.

As this was the only time I've ever seen or heard the story of the Bethel demon expanded as such, much of it is likely the invention of my former classmate or wherever he heard it from. Nevertheless, the graveyard remains tainted by rumors of this inexplicable beast with no origin.

Maybe, someday, more light can be shed or something new can develop out of it that could help uncover the mystery – after all, not all stories simply stop just because nothing has happened with them for several decades. Many legends adapt with the times where new theories can be made upon new discoveries, but whether they're inventions of the storytellers or not, they're always great stories to hear.

Phantoms in the Mountains

If there is a more majestic and awe-inspiring place in the Eastern United States than the Appalachian Mountains, I have yet to see it. I grew up in the foothills of the Tennessee Great Smoky Mountains, a sub-range of the Blue Ridge Mountains, and most of my life's scenery is painted with emerald greens for spring and summer, an explosion of color for fall, and a stoic, haunting gray and white for winter. I have been to the beaches of the East Coast, the Great Plains of the Midwest, even the Highlands of Scotland, and truly nothing I have ever seen on Earth compares to Appalachia. There is something genuinely mystic in these hills and plateaus – it is invisible and untouchable, but something is here that you can't find anywhere else.

The early settlers apparently thought so too. Ulster-Scot settlers started coming into the backcountry in the 18th century, seeking freedom from the governments, churches, and Quaker landowners that had harassed them, and fell in love with the familiarity of the mountains. With them came the many legends and spiritual concepts from the old country that were fused with the fears they faced in these new lands. It wouldn't be long before their mysticism started co-mingling with the mysticisms of the Native Americans, and their stories of demons and haunts held great seniority to what little the white settlers knew about these lands they were calling home.

27

Ghost stories come from fear and ignorance, and when you're moving a poor family to a mountain range that is just as new to civilized man as it is to you, you don't know what you might come across. Mountains mean caves, hiding places for beasts and thieves; dangerous terrain miles from any doctor and miles still from a helpful one; frozen winters, strange new animals eating your food supply, and, probably worst of all, very slow progress towards technology and information.

Even today, many of these problems are still a challenge for those who call Southern Appalachia home. Some areas are still completely inaccessible by modern vehicles, technology still seems to be six to twelve months behind in general (in my experiences, at least), and the unnerving feeling that something very dark and undiscovered hides out there, waiting to pounce on you the minute you trip over a rock, is still there. Figures and shadows drift around the hollows and make sounds that turn your blood to ice, bizarre things happen when no one else is around to see it and, because so much of the mountains remains hidden, you just never truly know what could be out there.

Here are just a few of the legends that linger like the mists of the peaks and valleys. We'll begin in the highlands of North Georgia.

* * * * *

Earl Johnson's Pig Parlor was the name of a farmhouse owned by a reputedly wealthy farmer in the northern mountains of Georgia during the early 20th century, and every Saturday evening it was where he and four of his good friends met every week, from 1916 to 1921, for a poker game.

Each of the five men was flush with cash from successful business ventures and reasonably well-known in the area, and it is said that, of the five, it was Earl that could be considered the local eccentric tycoon. While most people in the Appalachian Mountains would want a large family around to help work the land and provide much-needed company while living isolated up in the hills, Earl was apparently all by himself with no relatives that could be found. He also had no electricity, so his group had to play poker by the light of a few lanterns. Though electricity was hard to come by in the early part of that century, certainly a man with his money and means could find a way to bring it up there, yet, for some reason he chose to do without.

Finally, it was said that, like many eccentric tycoons with a touch of paranoia about them, Earl did not trust banks and kept all of his money somewhere at the Pig Parlor, obscured from prying eyes and away from any hands that didn't belong to him. Exactly why Earl wanted his lifestyle set up this way or how these rumors got started is not known, but they would all contribute to the horrifying demise that secured his legacy.

One Saturday night, as Earl and his four friends were enjoying a typical poker outing, the cards were on the table and moonshine was in their blood. A group of men, who might have heard the local gossip about the Pig Parlor and used it to plan a robbery, stormed the building and killed all five of the players.

The next day, the authorities arrived to a slaughterhouse – all five men weren't just lying on the floor dead, they were *decapitated*. Earl and his friends were attacked by someone ruthless enough to take the time and effort to behead five men just to get the money. Who these murderers were, and whether any secret stash was ever found will forever remain a mystery, and that will only be the *first* mystery of the Pig Parlor.

Some years later, as the farmhouse and property had decayed in its violent abandonment, people started reporting that strange lights were seen in the farmhouse on Saturday nights at the usual time the men had started their poker games. Kids and adults alike would go up to the old Pig Parlor, wait until 9:00PM or 10:00PM, and then see five lights shining in the dark – four lights from inside the farmhouse and one out on the deck, swinging a lantern. The ghosts of the five slain men apparently didn't even let death deter them from their weekly poker game.

According to the legend, it seems the one on the porch holding the lantern is actually the lookout for the other four so they won't be ambushed again... though what they could possibly be afraid of at this point is another mystery entirely.

* * * * *

From Georgia, we travel to another Southern mountain range that is famous for ghostly illuminations in Appalachian folklore. **The Brown Mountain Lights** of the Pisgah National Forest in Morganton, North Carolina have been sighted from areas like the Blue Ridge Parkway, Linville Falls, Green Mountain Overlook and Table Rock since they were first recorded by German engineer, Gerard Will de Brahm, in 1771. The Brown Mountain Lights are not just a legend that gets talked about whenever the subject of ghosts comes up in conversation; it is a cultural keystone of the mountains of North Carolina, having inspired folk songs, novels that link it to the extinction of the dinosaurs and even an episode of *The X-Files*.

The phenomena itself is puzzling enough; it is literally just a set of strange lights hovering over Brown Mountain on random, dark nights throughout the year. They appear in even more unpredictable fashions with some people seeing them as hazy orbs, slow-moving fireballs, or even as fireworks that pop in the air and burst out. They may be any color or any size and what to expect is to expect anything. They also don't seem to want anything other than to make a spectacle of themselves. Just where would something like this come from?

Well, there are two theories as to what they are, and they are not necessarily exclusive from each other. The first theory states the lights are the ghosts of Native Americans – either from an old, unnamed battle between the Cherokee and Catawba tribes, or from the wives, mothers and lovers that died waiting for them to come back from the fight and continue searching for them in death. The second theory, which is as old as 1850, states that the lights are the work of an undying spirit named Belinda who lived with her husband in the Brown Mountain area and may have been murdered by him. She just flatly disappeared one day, and the entire community began looking for her. It was around this time when the lights first started appearing, and the community began to wonder if it was a clue as to Belinda's whereabouts. When she didn't turn up, fingers were pointed to the husband, who conveniently left the area before accusations could get more serious. A skeleton of a woman was eventually found under a pile of rocks in a ravine on Brown Mountain, the lights returned again at night, and the legend was born.

It could be one theory or the other, both or neither as to the origins of the Brown Mountain Lights, but what we do know for sure is the impact of this phenomenon goes beyond a simple ghost story. So many people have reported them that the U.S. Geological Survey conducted two separate investigations on the matter. The first one in 1913 officially concluded the lights were reflected from a passing locomotive, but in 1916, this conclusion was challenged when a major flood went through the Catawba Valley and incapacitated the railroad tracks for a period of time. The lights were still seen. A second U.S.G.S investigation concluded the lights were the result of marsh gases spontaneously combusting at night, a conclusion that seems to be the government's official answer to anything paranormal and loses further credibility when one remembers that *there are no marshes* in Brown Mountain.

31

As the years past and more people and agencies became interested in the lights, more hypotheses were drawn up – ranging from reflections of moonshine distilleries and St. Elmo's Fire to even the possibility they are a *mirage* from the city lights surrounding the mountains, which seems particularly unlikely as they were first reported long before the surrounding cities even existed, much less the city lights.

As of this writing, the Brown Mountain Lights remain an unsolved wonder of the South and an excellent example of how folklore can evolve from a campfire story into a full-fledged sensation that people from all over visit to witness for themselves. Many do not leave disappointed.

* * * * *

If the folklore of Appalachian history is any authority on the simple mountain dwellers that lived for generations up in the hills, then we can conclude they were, and continue to be, a culture occasionally blessed with the powers of premonition. Open just about any book on Southern ghost lore and folktales, and a fourth of it may be dedicated to stories of odd elders and hereditary lines coming into contact with brief flashes of the future. Sometimes they would come as unexpected as a blizzard in July, and others were so used to them, it was hardly worth a passing word. Being humble as they were, the mountain folk who claim the power, on behalf of themselves or an old spinster aunt, just talked about them as if they were discussing a football game from twenty years ago. Maybe it wasn't a power they wanted to share – indeed, as a majority of premonitions are little more than forewarnings of impending death with almost no chance to stop them from happening, who would call it a blessing?

Ghosts are strangely married to legends of premonitions, and many stories feature the surprise image of a loved one

appearing at the door, on the street, or in a reflecti
carry a message, others let their appearances do the talking for
them, and neither is very clear most of the time. Then the next
day comes, and those who experience the premonition learn
that their loved one has passed away. Even stranger than that
are stories of premonitions where the loved ones' souls appear
to their families *before* they die, leading to many good
questions about what it was they actually saw. Clearly, it could
not have been the real spirit of the loved one, because they
were still alive when it appeared! What's going on here?

One of the most interesting stories of a premonition that I
have come across referred to the forecasting phantasm as a
Play Pretty. A play pretty is actually a very old word for a
common toy that was used in Texas during the early-to-mid
1900s, but the old spinster aunt who was visited by this
mysterious apparition seemed to consider it a play thing... at
first.

This story does not seem to indicate a specific region of
the mountains where it originated from, it simply tells the story
of the Waddell family's Great-Aunt Cynthia who was visited
by a strange and innocent-looking triangle of light she called
the "Play Pretty." It had started coming into her room at night
when she was in bed and danced around the room before
disappearing as curiously as it appeared. As the Waddell family
was a large body of people living under one big roof, several of
the children heard it and wanted to see it for themselves.
Cynthia agreed and for the next few nights, the children got to
see the Play Pretty for themselves.

Then one morning, Cynthia came to the breakfast table
and told the family the Play Pretty came into her room the
previous night, as it always had, but this time, instead of
leaving, it went to the center of the room and expanded in size
until she could see something coming out of it.

33

It was a coffin... with her name on it. Cynthia died three days later.

What makes premonition folklore particularly interesting, beyond the myriad of devices that come into contact with us, is that it is genuinely possible to experience a premonition of your own death before it happens. It is of a rare coincidental quality, but reports of people who dream of something happening only a short time before it actually occurs exist and could theoretically happen to anyone. Sometimes, it may be nothing more than a feeling about an object or place that just bothers a person until something really comes of it. A light version of this happened to my own former pastor, who found himself suddenly worried about something going on at the church one night. He became so disturbed by it that he drove down the mountain at 2:00AM to the church and found that a homeless man had broken in and was sleeping in the narthex.

Who knows how a society as proudly traditional and uncomplicated as the societies of southern Appalachia comes to possess powers like these? Maybe those old northerner conventions about us being a bunch of ignorant hicks aren't true after all. Even today, the rest of country tends to heckle the Southern mountain man for his simple thoughts and ways, but if you only knew what he knows, you wouldn't be laughing so hard...

* * * * *

It is difficult to imagine the history of the Southern Appalachian Mountains without conjuring images of the coal mining industries from the mid-19th and early 20th centuries. The United State experienced a huge industrial boon after the Civil War led by machines hungry for coal. Early settlers found and noted many ripe veins of coal in the vast Southern mountain ranges. Many other minerals, like gold, talc and copper, were eventually discovered as well, and mining corporations were just as eager to get their hands on them, too... at any cost.

But life as a miner was almost no life at all, and the history of mining is as dark as the energy source they dug for. It was virtually a prison for the crime of being impoverished as many poor families sent their patriarchs to dig for money, and they wouldn't be back home for months to years at a time... if at all. A miner in the old days worked seven days a week, ate and slept in the filthy conditions he worked in, and rested only when he needed his strength to mine some more. Safety regulations and workers' rights wouldn't be acknowledged for decades to come and management, at best, couldn't be trusted. When you put all that together, you have a recipe for disaster as unfocused, weak and sloppy men make mistakes that cost lives.

A mine is just about the purest, darkness place there is in the mountains, and so nearly every abandoned one that can be found is rumored to be haunted from top to bottom with the souls of dead miners who never made it back out. One of those is known simply as **The Cavern Near Plant #5** in Georgia, which has reports of several spirits wandering around the tunnels and surrounding hills.

One story recounts two mine workers who were working on a dozer very deep inside the mine. As they took a break, they saw a man coming towards them wearing a very different set of clothes than the rest of the men. He passed them and seemingly went about his business. The two workers did not recognize him and went to their supervisor to ask who he was. When they described him, the supervisor became pale with a wild look on his face. He knew the man they were describing... he had been crushed to death more than thirty years before.

Another rumor is that the deepest tunnel in the mine, one that had been closed off for years due to a cave-in, is haunted by the spirit of a worker who was killed when the rock came crashing down. Sounds of someone tapping against the rock from the inside reverberate throughout the tunnel walls and remind the men why even the bravest and toughest of them refuse to ever go down there.

A much stranger report happened outside The Cavern one night to a miner's wife. This miner worked a shift so late that his lunch whistle went off at 2:00AM. His wife often got up with him and prepared his lunch, but this particular night he was in a hurry and accidentally left his lunch behind. His wife then drove up the mountain to deliver it to him, and as she got closer to the entrance, she started to feel very scared without knowing why... until she got to the top of the road, over the railroad tracks, and looked into the valley below. The entire area beneath her was enshrouded by a green mist that twisted, turned and warped itself. It looked like a large cluster of spirits. The details of this particularly disturbing account end there, but it would beg the following questions – was that a congregation of those who had died inside the plant, or was it a different entity altogether that could be fueling the disturbances in the area? Ghosts roaming around the mountains are quite common occurrences in folklore, but to come across a whole shroud of them covering the entire lowland is a different story altogether, from which no good can come.

This point was illustrated by one more shocking report that nearly ended in disaster. A man was operating a dump truck while his companion was operating a bulldozer until he hit a tunnel wall. As the other man came to help, they both saw the wall collapse and reveal a hidden cave behind it. They went inside to look and saw a number of crosses stuck into the ground. These were gravesites, but for who? Why would someone bury a number of people inside the mine and then hide it behind a cavern wall?

But before they could look closer to find some clues for this mystery, the bulldozer behind them started up on its own and started moving toward them. One of the men rushed onto it to turn it off, but could not stop the machine. The other man was frozen in fear and just barely managed to get out of the way. The two got outside the gravesite and watched the bulldozer plow through the crosses and into the rear wall, causing the entire hidden cave to collapse. Whatever was inside there did not want to be discovered, and was willing to kill just so it could remain locked away from the world.

Whether any of these reports connect to reveal a very dark presence inside the mine is up for speculation, but not conclusion. Some things in history are probably better left undiscovered, and if stories alluding to the true depth of the mining tragedies in the South are as ghastly as these, we may not want to tread any further.

* * * * *

Near the eastern coast of North Carolina we come to another mountain range saturated with the supernatural. The Uwharrie Mountains of Davidson, Montgomery, Randolph and Stanly counties (with foothills stretching into four more) may be the quintessential image of the old-time Appalachian Mountain community – raised on folklore, sharing ghost stories of old and personal accounts of the disembodied visitors that sometimes drop by. Over three dozen stories have been accounted out of the Uwharries and here are two that perfectly capture the spirit of Southern ghost lore in the highlands.

One old soul who used to sit on his porch and share stories was a man by the name of **Abraham Shadd**, who lived near the foot of Lick Mountain and Haw Branch, and was a favored member of that community when was alive. Abraham had a warm personality and made many friends in the mountains through his work with two pioneer doctors that migrated to the Uwharries. Although Abraham was not a medical practitioner, he was a major asset to the doctors' operations as he tended to the horses, the wagons, the vegetable garden, the house and its many repair needs, and occasionally assisted the doctors if two sets of hands weren't enough to help a patient. It was good, honest work for a good, honest man and Abe was happy to do it.

But that was only the side of their operations that the community saw. Underneath that surface was a far more macabre operation keeping their medical practice afloat, because once the sun went down, the three would literally moonlight as grave robbers – poaching for fresh corpses in soft burial grounds, bringing bodies back to the farmhouse, and stripping them down to skeletons clean enough to sell as demonstration dummies to medical schools.

For many nights across many years, the three would move in the silence of darkness toward any of the graveyards that were nearby and start looking for the easiest tomb to defile. Once they had what they came for, the corpse was replaced with weighted logs and the burial plot carefully re-planted and rearranged so no one could find any trace that they were ever there. When they got back to the farmhouse, the body was taken down to a secret workshop and boiled in a special metal vat until the skeletal figure was ready to be preserved. After that treatment was finished, it was packed up in a large box, sometimes even in the original casket, with very heavy padding, labeled "medical supplies" so no one would be suspicious, and shipped to any number of the buyers they came into contact with. It was a perfect system that went on for decades, and even though they had some close calls a number of times, amazingly, they were never caught.

So what would possess three well-respected men in the community to do something so ghastly for such a long time?

Money, of course. In those days, selling "medical supplies" was a far more lucrative industry than administering them to the living. Whether the doctors were amoral frauds trying to make an easy fortune or just trying to get more money for their practice to better serve the community is not known, but the fact remains that, no matter what their intentions were, their actions would have sparked outrage in the God-fearing community. In the South, you do *not* disrespect the dead. You take off your hat when someone speaks of them, you slow down during a funeral procession, and you do *not* pluck them out of the ground to make money off their humble remains. Had they been exposed, they might have been burned at the stake.

Abraham, at least, was still a conscientious man and he did his best to operate as a good, honest worker under those circumstances. Abraham stayed at Haw Branch, having acquired the deed to the former medical farmhouse (some say to help buy his silence on their dealing) and spending much of the rest of his life doing odd jobs for his friends and neighbors. He very much felt the impact of his work with the doctors and it probably weighed very heavy on his mind.

When Abraham got too old to do much else, he started telling his story to anyone dropping by for a visit, but his stories often added that the spirits of the bodies he helped to exhume often came back to visit or pester him on a daily basis. He was even said to regularly converse with the spirit of old **Preacher Dandy Lucas**, who kept him up to date on what those medical skeletons were doing now as if he were talking about living people.

Abraham himself didn't live long into those years, and he is said to also be roaming around the area... still chatting with Dandy Lucas or any of the other spirits that he came to be acquainted with.

* * * * *

Another story from the Uwharries is a much darker tale of the hardships families had to endure before the new eras of Appalachian living could replace the old ones. Stories like **The Hearse Wagon** often describe in very fine, morbid detail how these mountain lifestyles could quickly fall apart when tragedy strikes.

Cromer and Cora Calvert lived like most reasonably normal couples did in the Uwharries in the old days. Cromer was a mountain man through and through and could often be found hunting and roaming the hills as he pleased. There was no more satisfying lifestyle in the entire world as far as Cromer was concerned, and he found time to enjoy it even as Cora produced children for them to raise. Life was good for the Calvert home in the mountains.

Then, one day, as Cromer and Cora were in their middle years, Cora became sick with an incurable illness, and all the doctor could do for them was advise Cromer to make his wife's last days as comfortable as possible. Cromer was heartbroken, like any man would be, but his heart was torn into two halves for two loves: his wife and his hobbies, and he could not be there for both.

To make it even more unfortunate, Cora's illness was very slow to claim her life, but quick to deteriorate her from a sprightly and lovely woman into a bedridden shadow of her former self. Her mind raced with the fears of death. Her personality turned arsenic and unreasonable, abusing Cromer for any reason she could find, lashing out at the children and the neighbors who visited to try to brighten her day, and making absolutely sure that everyone around her was as miserable as she was. She would often wake up screaming in fear that the "hearse wagon" was coming to get here any day now. Once a free man who could hunt, hike and explore as much as he wanted, now Cromer was a prisoner to this vile husk that used to be his wife and he knew that he could be chained to her for several years.

The thought of catering to this slowly suffering woman eventually became too much for Cromer to bear, and he took matters into his own hands by smothering Cora with her pillow until both their agonies ceased. It was a struggle, and the last thing Cora gasped before she died was an oath that, someday, the hearse wagon would come for him too.

Her funeral came and went without anyone suspecting Cromer of foul play. Not long after her death, he resumed his activities in the mountains, overjoyed for the shackles to be broken at last. He only enjoyed them for a short time however; not long after his wife had uttered her final curse, Cromer started hearing noises outside the house that sounded like a wagon pulling up to the door, waiting for a few minutes, and then speeding away. Many late evenings, Cromer would hear, as clear as day, something pulling up to the door, but he would never see anything. Interestingly enough, other visitors who stayed with Cromer also heard the sounds of a wagon driving through without ever seeing it.

Cromer's life continued on a slow, downward spiral for which he never recovered. In his loneliness, he married Cora's younger sister (so young, in fact, she was apparently able to produce him a new brood of children) and this at least kept him from losing himself completely to despair as he grew older. Even that was be short-lived as he, too, became ravaged with illness that twisted him from the inside and out. He became a bitter husk just like Cora. The hearse sounds continued all the while and he knew that any one of those nights, it was going to stop... and when it did, it wasn't going to leave without him.

Finally, one night, the infernal clomping of the otherworldly coach became so loud that Cromer suffered an anxiety attack while his second wife was preparing his pillow and collapsed on the floor, having succumbed at long last to his first wife's curse. The sound of the ghostly wagon was heard driving out of the yard, and this time, it would be gone for good.

* * * * *

Speaking of the devil, it may not come as a shock to learn that he has been constantly reported to be haunting hundreds of areas in the Southern Appalachia since the earliest of the pioneer days; so much so, in fact that one has to wonder if he owns real estate somewhere around there. Trying to figure out why he would want to keep appearing to harass the simple mountain folk of the Bible Belt is a fairly futile exercise for something so gnarled and depraved. There is no point in trying to figure him out – you just need to be prepared in case he comes looking for you. The story of **The Cutter Legend** seems to suggest that even when you do know how to handle the devil, he may win all the same.

The Cutter Legend comes from the mountains of North Georgia and begins shortly before 1904 when a seventeen-year-old girl named Sarah Cutter married a local boy named Grady Watson. Sarah's family was very tight-knit, highly religious, and into the moonshining business to put food on the table. A cabin was built near the Cutter family to keep them both close by, but such proximity gave Grady ample opportunity to indulge heavily in their moonshine and he became an abusive drunk both to his wife, and a baby son born in 1905. Sarah could only take so much before she took their child and moved back in with her parents.

Sarah's father, Hoyt Cutter, was understandably upset, but he felt it was his Christian duty to go down and pray for Grady, and so he took his son and Sarah's brother, Rainey, down with him to help get Grady straight with the Lord and back on the right path... little did they know he was already literally dancing down a much different one at that very time.

Just before they reached his cabin, Hoyt and Rainey started hearing bizarre, guttural screams and what sounded like cursing and freaking out. Something was clearly wrong. When they found Grady, he was dancing in a jig with a look of violence and horror on his face while he screamed in a highly disturbed fashion. He looked like he was tearing at something that had jumped on him from behind. They couldn't see it at first, but when he moved into the moonlight, they saw what was attacking him – a faceless figure that rode him like a horse and commanded him to dance... the devil himself.

Hoyt shouted for Rainey to get on his knees and the two immediately began praying. Their prayers were rapid, and just when they thought the horrible sounds and screeching would last an eternity, everything suddenly stopped. Both men looked up and found Grady and the devil were gone.

The next day, they called the sheriff's office for help in locating Grady. When the sheriff and his men arrived, they set out at the last site Grady was seen at with two bloodhound dogs. They looked inside the cabin and found everything in disarray. No trace of Grady was recovered and the dogs themselves were positively spooked once they found the spot where he had been dancing. They picked up a sense of something evil that was still there, and refused to go any further. Once the sheriff and the bloodhounds left, Hoyt and Rainey burned down the cabin, as if to completely remove any lasting impressions the boy ever existed. Grady was gone and he would never been seen again.

The night Grady disappeared was October 31st, 1905. In those days, it was believed Halloween night was when the devil went scouring for souls to take back to Hell, and those that know the legend conclude that Grady just happened to be ripe for the picking that night.

* * * * *

The devil's mischievous influence doesn't end there. It has been rumored for decades that he owns property in both Carolinas known as **The Devil's Tramping Grounds,** or sometimes alternately known as **The Devil's Stomping Grounds**. For the sake of clarity, we'll refer to the mysterious ring in Chatham County, North Carolina as the "Tramping Grounds" and the one in Lancaster County, South Carolina as the "Stomping Grounds."

Both legends refer to a unique circle of dead earth where the devil is said to dance at night. The very laws of nature are warped inside each circle – nothing will grow; no ants, worms or spiders will be found inside; no sound can be heard from inside the circle; there is an intense assault of negative emotion when you get inside it; and if you leave objects inside the circle overnight, by morning it will kicked outside by the devil himself as he dances. Both rings are also said to have existed since the days of the Native Americans who used each ring for different purposes. In North Carolina, it is said the local tribes used it to hold tribal ceremonies and dances. The South Carolina circle's legend goes further, suggesting the Stomping Grounds were the execution sites for both the Catawba and the Waxaw tribes and that evil spirits also gather there to collect more souls for eternal condemnation.

The stories surrounding the blighted patches make up a very loose mythology, and there are further claims to the legend that are inconsistent and borderline ludicrous. As I researched it, I found that one person even alleged that he and a group camped inside the Tramping Grounds circle and were all separated in morning... with one person found more than a *mile* away! Even in this realm of study, that is a very extraordinary

44

claim, usually something you would hear reported on the news if it really happened.

It may be that The Devil's Tramping and Stomping Grounds fit more the mold of an urban legend, which can be similar to ghost lore, but may have certain elements of its mythological makeup that can be tested to verify claims. In this case, there are more definite parameters to the legend, as opposed to a haunted house where the ghost of a woman may appear in one of several forms in any part of the house on the occasional night *if* she feels like it, one could actually go to either the Tramping or Stomping Grounds and see if these abnormalities truly operate on a regular basis.

In 2011, a college group from Elon University in North Carolina set out to do just that. Two groups went out to test a majority of the major claims about the Tramping Ground and found that:

1. The ring being cleaned before daybreak is *completely false*.
2. The ring being incapable of growing vegetation is *completely false*.
3. The ring being completely deaf at night is *completely false*.
4. The ring being trampled by the devil himself is *likely false*, as one subgroup *did* hear footsteps they could not easily explain while another subgroup did not hear any.

And while the The Devil's Tramping and Stomping Grounds being distant twins might seem like a unique quality that adds more authenticity to the legend, to some at least, the truth is that there are similar ones all over the country – there is one fitting that description much further south in Lake County, Florida, for a start. In fact, compiled volumes of natural phenomena show that strange circles have been pervasive in

45

human history for centuries. The crop circle craze that started in the mid-20th century is the most immediate thing that may come to mind, but even before that were reports of perfectly round discs of ice forming randomly in frozen bodies of water that spun slightly on their own accord. The devil's fascination with circles even appears in an early account from Herefordshire, England in the summer of 1678 when a farmer quarreled with his hired hand over a payment for cutting his crops. The farmer refused to pay his asking price and said he would rather the devil himself do the job. That night, a red, fiery glow was seen in his field, and the next day there were perfect circles cut into his crops. A woodcut of that scene called the "mowing devil" became quite famous.

All the same, the two rings make for a great ghost story to tell late at night and many kids who hear about them at friends' houses or scout trips often remember them fondly. While it's important to separate fact from story in any serious inquiry to the subject, folklore today isn't about facts, it's about fun. It's fun to hear stories about real life places with fantasy realms hidden somewhere in there.

And in the mountains, there is no shortage of hidden realms waiting to be discovered by an unassuming traveler who has no idea what he or she might be in store for...

Haunted Highways & Spectral Streets

In the days before automobiles were mass-produced and became as essential to own and maintain as a house, travel in the southern part of the country could be a horribly tedious and dangerous fixture of daily life. With huge tracts of land in the Southern states and extremely long roads connecting them, going between cities in the same state could take days under the best of weather conditions by horse and buggy. If you didn't have a buggy, you had to go saddleback and maintain both the horse and yourself all along the way. Some people, particularly those in the mountains when roads were slow to come, had access to neither and foraged to the general stores on foot. If Pa left to get supplies for the winter, he might not be seen until later in the week.

Even if you had a horse and buggy, you could still be in big trouble if you were ambushed by thieves in a tunnel or covered pathway, if a wheel came off while you were miles and miles away from any destination that could help you, or if you got caught in a storm with no adequate shelter nearby. Road and driving conditions started improving dramatically by the mid-20th century, but then there were new problems to face – drunk drivers, unsafe or incomplete roads (again, particularly those in the mountains) and new breeds of criminals to watch out for.

Danger and tragedy are never too far away from the roads here in the South... and where there is danger and tragedy, there is a volume of ghost lore.

Almost every street and recognizable road of the South seems to have a spirit attached to it, but probably more so than other branches of ghost lore, the stories surrounding them follow a fairly narrow set of conventions, and, as such, carbon copies of haunted sharp turns ("dead man's curve"), bridges where, under certain circumstances, you can hear a baby crying ("crybaby bridge"), and long stretches of road where a "vanishing hitchhiker" might beckon for a ride appear all over the country, even as far as Hawaii! Many of these stories qualify as local urban legends as a result, but many others have fascinating and unique histories of their own as well.

As we spent much of the previous chapter in Georgia and North Carolina, we'll see what Alabama, Kentucky and South Carolina have to offer us in this one. Let's have a look...

* * * * *

Montgomery, of the eponymous county in Alabama, is the capital city of the state with a long history of growth and cultural accomplishments for the South. It is the birthplace of Nat King Cole and Big Mama Thornton, and the city where Hank Williams Sr. got his start to a legendary career. Montgomery was the first city in the U.S. to install electric street cars for public transit as far back as 1886, and an important city for the civil rights movements of the mid-20th century where Rosa Parks was arrested in 1955 for refusing to give her bus seat to a white man, and where the famous "Selma-to-Montgomery Marches" took place in 1965.

With a city as historically significant as Montgomery, it follows there would be ghost stories that circulate well-known halls and buildings. Huntingdon College is haunted by the spirits of **The Red Lady** and **The Ghost On The Green**, both victims of suicide, the **Tallapoosa Entertainment Center** casino is supposedly built on a Native American burial ground, the **Maxwell Air Force Base** has shadows that wander the student dorms and randomly soak sleeping cadets, and even the **State Capitol Building** itself is said to have a Confederate woman that wanders the halls and turns on the bathroom water faucets for no apparent purpose.

And then you have stories coming from areas around the city that are not as well-known, but considerably more interesting. The legend of **The Thirteen Bridges** is one of them. Now known as Barganier Road and located just outside the city of Montgomery in Cecil, Alabama, the former Thirteen Bridges Road was named quite literally after the thirteen little bridges that went over creeks and lakes and was rumored to be a place where thugs and gang members sometimes hung out.

It is said that the bridges are haunted by the spirits of a woman and her child who died in a car accident after driving over the bridges. Supposedly, you can count thirteen bridges going through the pass one way, but only twelve bridges going back. On some nights, like Halloween, you may even hit something that looks like a dog. When you go outside to check on it, it will appear dead and then the woman and her child will appear to you in the distance. Then the dog will suddenly get up, dart towards the thirteenth bridge and disappear with it, leaving only twelve bridges. The canine spirit is the dog that caused the car accident in the first place and died along with the woman and child. Another variation has it in reverse, saying that you will only count twelve bridges going across the first time, and the thirteenth one will appear, covered in a strange mist, when you go back. If you look into the mist as you cross it, you will see the face of a girl who died there and she will try to pull you into the water.

49

Another reported experience was that, years ago, a teenage boy moved to Montgomery, Alabama, and was introduced to the legend as a local test of bravery. The boy and a friend took a car to get there and the boy was to stand on the bridge for five minutes. As he stood there, he slowly became overwhelmed by the presence of something he couldn't identify. When he turned to look for his friend, both he and the car were gone. The car couldn't have left on its own as the gravel grinding under the tires is too loud to not notice it leaving. The boy went off to look for the car and found that it was back on the other end of the bridges – in fact, the car had never left... it was the same bridge he had stood on previously. Somehow, he had moved from one end of the road to the other without noticing it.

Sadly, (or thankfully), the former Thirteen Bridges road is closed, likely due to the sad shape of the bridges and the increased traffic from curious kids and seedy individuals who usually gravitate towards those sites, but the legend and its bizarre experiences grow to this day.

* * * * *

From Alabama, we move east to find a little town known as Gaffney, South Carolina, the county seat of Cherokee County. Also known as the "Peach Capital of South Carolina," Gaffney is named after an Irish emigrant who came to the area in 1804 and established an inn and tavern known as "Gaffney's Cross Roads" which soon grew into "Gaffney City" in 1872. Before the turn of the 20th century, Gaffney City became a backbone for the textile industries of South Carolina and stayed that way for more than eighty years.

But beneath the peach trees and that brief, positive description of a happy little town is a thick layer of darkness inside its history. The citizens of Gaffney were attacked by two serial killers in two different eras – in 1968 by Lee Roy Martin, the "Gaffney Strangler," and in 2009 by spree killer Patrick Tracy Burris. Lee was a serial killer with a split personality, according to interviews he gave in prison, and between 1967 and 1968, he had murdered four women, with the husband of one of them being falsely convicted of the murder, while he worked at a local mill and had a family of his own. He was ultimately stabbed to death in prison in 1972. Patrick Burris, on the other hand, was a major repeat criminal with a list of offenses reported to be more than twenty-five pages in length. His motive remains unknown as his victims ranged across the board: males and females, both young and old, fell to this man for seemingly no reason, and his spree only ended when he did during a police shootout in Dallas, North Carolina.

At least two sites are said to be haunted by the victims of Lee Roy Martin. There is a road called **Chain Gang Hill Road**, which was apparently a "lover's lane" road at one point, about ten miles away in Spartanburg that is said to be haunted by some of the women he murdered, and you can hear their voices as they moan and scream together in the dark of night. But, why there would be multiple ghosts there when only one of his victims was found at that site? It is a good question to ask anyone sharing the legend. The next road that is said to be the eternal prison of his victims, **U.S. Highway 329**, is more believable in the context of ghost logic, claiming only one spirit – his second victim, Nancy Parris, who was found underneath the bridge. She is also said to still be calling for help and howling in pain throughout the night.

And then there is *another* road near Gaffney that has long been held to superstition since 1979. **Booger Jim** is the name of the ghost haunting U.S. Highway 29, which connects Gaffney to Blacksburg. Jim was said to be a local drunk who would find himself sleeping under the bridge after one of many binges throughout any given week. Presumably, he did not want to go home to his wife, by name of Becca, while under the influence... and given what she did when she couldn't tolerate his alcoholism any longer, he had every reason to worry. She is said to have hung him off the bridge, in a fit of rage, with a set of *jumper cables.*

His ghost is said to appear if you walk onto the bridge (itself an impressive feat considering it is a narrow-lane bridge with constant traffic) and call his name three times. He may appear as a shadow, as a full-color visage of his former self with a rope burn on his throat, or even as a figure that is half-man and half-cow! The latter appearance was most likely a facetious invention to an already unbelievable tale, but to this day, many go to the bridge, braving traffic, to try summoning Booger Jim and see which appearance they might get.

There are three more sites in Gaffney rumored to be haunted, including yet another bridge frequented by the shade of a woman with a basket. There are no hauntings currently associated with the victims of Patrick Burris, but in ten or fifteen years' time, that may very well change...

* * * * *

There is a surprising statistic regarding modern teenage drivers – only six out of ten teenagers have their license as opposed to eight out of ten some thirty years ago, according to a study conducted by the University of Michigan in July of 2012. This shift, which might go as far as to shock many who remember the days when they couldn't wait to get their driving licenses as teenagers, comes as the American lifestyle and the world at large morph into unknown shapes due to a high dependence on current networking technology, a stuttering and unpredictable economy, and what some people consider a "coddling" of the current generation.

It used to be a cultural pastime and a fundamental fact of life that teenagers of every size and shape waited from the onset of puberty to sweet sixteen with bated breath for the coveted laminate card. It was the first true step to independence and adulthood. The attitude was that they could go wherever they want, as fast as they want, and wouldn't have to answer to anyone... until they got busted speeding or cruising with the sleazebag boyfriend/girlfriend that their parents disapproved of. Indeed, they often learned the hard way that they had to create places where they could explore their newfound sense of freedom without getting hassled by their folks or the cops, so they came up with hangout spots where they could race, make-out, and further "explore" the joys of adulthood. **Hot Rod Haven** in Louisville, Kentucky is one of those places.

Mitchell Hill Road is the official name of the road the teenagers used to call Hot Rod Haven and from the 1940s to the 1970s. If you wanted to prove your manhood, you raced down that dangerous road with another local hooligan while fans cheered you on. It was a very popular spot for teenagers but also very dangerous, as it had a wild selection of twists and sharp turns snaking through the woods. Upwards of twenty-five deaths had been reported from between those decades and two of them, a pair of adolescents who fell victim to Hot Rod Haven, have long been rumored to still be roaming the street.

The traditional version of the back-story to the haunting on Mitchell Hill Road goes that, in September of 1950, a car crash claimed the life of a young woman, name of either Sarah or Mary Mitchell, and her boyfriend, a boy by the name of Roy Clarke, as they missed a turn and drove right off the hill. It was said that they were buried at the top of the hill next to each other, with members of their family going so far as planning to be buried next to them on that same hill to honor them. Sarah or Mary's grave is marked by a statue of an angel.

Years later, the director of the Louisville Ghost Hunters Society went to verify the facts in the story and found that, yes, there are two grave markers on Mitchell Hill Road for a Sarah Mitchell and Roy Clarke, buried side-by-side. Before that, he found that Sarah Mitchell and Roy Clarke were high school students who died on Mitchell Hill Road, but the details of it were completely different. It was September of 1946 and the two were actually on their way to a school dance when Roy lost control of his car and crashed. In terms of folklore, this is an interesting find where the details of the back-story are false, yet still lead up to proving the conclusion is true.

As a result of that tragedy, strange things are said to occur on the road, with travelers reporting a ghostly girl wandering around the gravesite in her dance dress and that pictures taken on the road will sometimes come back with strange orbs in the background. In the years following their deaths, when the legend was growing, teenage drag-racers used to go to Sarah's angel statue on the rumor that if you touch its arms, and they were cold, it would foretell that someone was to die during the race (this meant that many kids likely chickened out of racing, forgetting that stone statues are usually rather cold to touch anyway).

But the strangest legend that comes from Hot Rod Haven does not appear to have any connection to any of the deaths that occurred on the road, and may exist as a dark and perverse conglomeration of the residual spirits and energies left behind by those who were killed by Mitchell Hill's unforgiving bends and unsecured ridges. There is a car that occasionally appears, without warning, behind very scared drivers who know there wasn't a car there just a moment ago. It only turns its lights on to flash the driver before disappearing as mysteriously as it appeared. If they happen to be driving on a bad night, it will even try to run them off the road just because it feels like doing so. Either driven by an evil spirit, or an evil spirit manifesting as a vehicle itself, this car does nothing but add more danger to a road that has already claimed at least twenty-five lives in recent memory.

If there is anything we don't need more of on our roads, danger is one of them. With so much to worry about on the highways and alleys already, maybe today's teenagers are actually quite sensible to wait longer to experience the roads for themselves – after all, if it hadn't been for reckless teenagers all those years ago giving kids behind the wheel such a bad image today, state laws and car insurance companies wouldn't be as quick to make it even harder for them to drive in the first place.

History can teach us surprising ironies sometimes.

* * * * *

From Kentucky, we return to Alabama and visit a town well-known for its driving – Talladega of NASCAR® fame. Its legacy comes from the **Talladega Superspeedway** motorsports complex, which regularly hosts the Nationwide Series (the NASCAR® equivalent of the minor league), the Camping World Series (modified pickup truck racing), and the most important NASCAR® racing series of the year: the Sprint Cup Series. For many who are not stockcar racing fans, the word Talladega brings to mind *Talladega Nights: The Ballad of Ricky Bobby*, a comedy movie that affectionately parodies the sport (to describe it generously) and some aspects of modern Southern culture in general. While the city is known outside the stockcar racing scene for the Talladega National Forest edging on the southern tip of the Appalachian Mountains and the Alabama Institute for the Deaf and Blind, the lifeblood of Talladega runs on four wheels with pistons pumping, engines flaring, and cars flying at over 200MPH.

It would be disappointing, then, if we didn't find any ghost stories associated with driving in this part of Alabama.

In fact, the Talladega Superspeedway is said to be cursed due to its unusual history and its penchant for fatal freak accidents. "Talladega" is actually a Muscogee/Creek Native American word that designated the area as a border town between the Muscogee and Natchez territories. It is said that the grounds beneath the hallowed racing oval are either ancient Native American burial ground, or the site where the Creeks were defeated in a skirmish with Andrew Jackson in 1813. The latter origin further states that one of the shamans of the conquered tribe uttered a curse on the land just before he died. Either way, the soil is said to be filled with dead men who do not appreciate being disturbed from their eternal rest by the sounds of racing cars and racing fans.

In 1968, "Big" Bill France, the co-founder of NASCAR®, broke ground in Alabama on what was to be an ambitious new racing track, one that was even bigger than Daytona. Bill was a man who could be quite stubborn when he wanted to be, and some versions of the legend say he was even warned the land was cursed before he began construction. Bill ignored the superstitious detractors and resumed work until the construction was finished a year later. The track opened on September 1969, but it wouldn't be until 1973 that those who had heard about the curse started wondering if something of that was beginning to stir on the racetrack. That year alone, Talladega saw a massive wreck during the Winston 500 that took out twenty-one cars and ended the career of Wendell Scott (the first African American to receive a NASCAR® racing license), the death of Larry Smith (Rookie of the Year in 1972) in a crash against the retaining wall, and a strange event in which Bobby Isaac quit in the middle of a race and subsequently retired as soon as the race was over... because he heard a voice in his head tell him to do so.

The years that followed into the modern era were punctuated with more bizarre catastrophes. In 1975, one of Richard Petty's pit crew members, who also happened to be his brother-in-law, was killed when a pressurized water tank he was carrying to extinguish a fire in Richard's car exploded, killing him instantly and launching his corpse into the air. In 1983, Phil Parsons and Darrell Waltrip accidentally started off an eleven-car chain crash that sent one vehicle flying and *somersaulting* until it landed on a car being driven by Ricky Rudd (that car was actually put in the Talladega Hall of Fame Museum as an example of the car wrecks they see). In 1987, "something" went underneath Bobby Allison's car as he was driving and blew out his tire with such force that the force of the combustion shot him nose-up into the sky, flipped him *backwards*, and into the catch-fence where spectators were struck by debris. In 2006, two spectators were electrocuted while setting up a metal flagpole in the campgrounds that came into contact with the high voltage wires overhead. Both were killed.

These are just a few of the extremely dangerous accidents that have occurred in the history of the Talladega Superspeedway, and while it would be quite natural to dismiss them all as very reasonable consequences for an excessively competitive sport featuring dozens of high-powered machines going over 200MPH, it should also be noted that racers with lucrative careers in front of them do not just suddenly decide to retire because of a "feeling," and cars do not just suddenly leap from the track into the audience because something made its way under the tire. Thankfully, these events are few and far between, weakening the credibility of any curse that might be transpiring, but as NASCAR® shows no signs of slowing down, and it's been a while since something that unbelievable has happened during a race, who knows what might happen on the track in the next few years?

And while there isn't much in the way of explicitly ghostly activity on the Superspeedway itself, there are actually several more places in the area rumored to be haunted. Talladega National Forest, as mentioned above, has Cemetery Road out of Sycamore where the dead, who are buried in the grounds surrounding the road, are said to be seen wandering the woods at night. In Munford, there is a church named **Bethlehem Methodist** where, if you drive around it three times, park in the front parking lot, face the church and turn off your lights, the blinds in the windows will raise by themselves and a yellow orb will rise from the cemetery across McElderry Road. Then there is a **Gravity Hill** not far from there on Cheaha Road where you can put your car in neutral and wait to be pulled up the mountain by a mysterious force. It is also said you said that you can hear the ghost of a murdered woman scream off in the distance as you're getting "towed."

Suffice to say, if you plan on going to Talladega anytime soon, you might want to ask your local priest to bless both you and your car before making the trip. It might be embarrassing to ask, but it could make all the difference in the world behind the steering wheel.

* * * * *

It would almost be criminal to dedicate an entire chapter to the supernatural mysteries of the Southern roads in the United States and not mention at least one ghostly hitchhiker legend. Hitchhiking has, is, and always will be, one of the most dangerous forms of social transportation you can find in modern society. You basically have to trust your life to a complete stranger sitting only inches away from you for upwards of several hours, possibly carrying a weapon or drugs, in a small, enclosed and very private space, inside a vehicle going 50MPH where the slightest venture off the paved path could mean injury or death for multiple parties. If your new travel partner isn't sane and sober from head to toe, you could really be in trouble.

With thousands of stories of ghosts reaching for rides in the dark of night scattered throughout the South, I went looking for a story that was a unique cut above the rest.

And boy, did I get it.

In Carter County of Tennessee is Gap Creek Road where a lurching ghoul known as the **Double-Headed Hitchhiker** is sometimes seen on the side of the street, hunched over and waiting for you to pass so he can grab onto your vehicle. Even if you've heard of a ghost with a name like that in Carter County, you would not be prepared for the frightening image that beckons for you as he is said to be 7ft. tall, with strong, lanky limbs, wearing either a strange, almost antique stovepipe hat (like President Lincoln used to have) or, as he gets his name, a second head that actually sits on top of the first one like the start of some hideous human totem pole.

This figure inspires multiple levels of fear and he hasn't even touched the car yet. As a hitchhiker, he falls very squarely into the *extreme* category and he will try to ride with you whether you let him or not. Even slowing down is not recommended because you will need all the speed your engine can afford if you want to outrun him. Most cars are able to beat his swift foot speed, but not all. For those unlucky drivers that hear his mutant paws scraping against the metal body, they find he has already latched on and is climbing over top of the car. From there, two bloody hands press down against the driver and passenger side windows as he looks inside from above, paralyzing the motorist with terror and, even worse, obstructing the view of the road like he's begging for a crash. Finally, the Double-Headed Hitchhiker cannot be thrown off once he's on. He wants his ride and your life will come a very distant second to that.

What horrible event in Carter County's history could have possibly happened to create something this twisted and aggressive? Why would it be so tenacious in catching such an unconventional ride when thousands of other ghosts are able to do just fine the old fashioned way?

The story goes that the Double-Headed Hitchhiker was once a young man by the name of Jubal growing up in Gap Run in the late 1920s. He had an older brother named James who decided, one day in 1928, to get married to the best girl the county had to offer. To do this, he purchased a Ford Model A and had it delivered by train from Michigan in time for the annual Fourth of July festival in Big Spring, an unincorporated community nearby that held big Independence Day celebrations every year. It was customary in those days to go in costume and Jubal, who is said to have resembled Abraham Lincoln with his tall, gangly frame, went with the obvious choice for his costume.

To get into character, Jubal dressed all in black, shaped his beard to befit the iconic President, and topped it off with a stovepipe hat that made him seem even taller than he was. His grandfather approved of the costume and gave Jubal a gold pocket watch that he received during the Civil War to complete the ensemble. With Honest Abe back in the flesh, it was time to ride in James' Model A to the big party.

The brothers had the times of their lives at the festival. James did not have to look too hard to find the girl that made his heart explode like the fireworks in the sky above, and while he was quickly making his moves on her, Jubal was having fun posing for pictures and acting in-character as Lincoln with his gold watch, on its heavy gold chain, persistently displayed out in his hand for all to see. As the night wore on, James was already set to marry the girl he just met and he asked for Jubal to walk home so they could have the car to themselves. Jubal agreed, and once the festival started winding down, he set out to get home by Gap Creek Road.

But Jubal never made it home. He was attacked by a homeless man with a knife that had likely seen the gold watch that Jubal flaunted at the festival and demanded it in exchange for his life. Jubal did not give up the watch and instead fought back, foolishly trying to grab at the knife in his assailant's hands. He was stabbed in the chest and back during the fight and once he realized he could not win, Jubal tried to flee for the road and hope someone passing by could get him to safety.

Miraculously, there *was* a car coming down the road – James' car. Thinking this was his lucky ticket out of this mess, Jubal reached out to the Model A coming over the curve. He hoped his brother would slow down and let him latch on, but James never slowed down. In fact, he pretended not to see his brother at all while his new sweetheart was in the car with him, thinking the Lincoln impersonator was drunk.

Watching his only chance to survive drive off was the last thing Jubal ever saw. The homeless man caught up to him and stabbed him once more in the heart. Once Jubal collapsed to the ground, the homeless man gleefully took the gold watch, seeing as how the young man wouldn't need it where he was going.

The very sad and desperate end that didn't have to happen reportedly corrupted Jubal's immortal soul, and it is said that decades of despair over that horrible night turned him into the frightening freak he is today... pathologically trying to tag on to any vehicle now in the eternal hope of getting his gold watch back and riding as far away from where he was murdered as he can.

But wait, how did he get to be known as the *Double-Headed* Hitchhiker then? Where did his second head come from? It is said the stovepipe hat is what confuses people into thinking he has two heads, but this explanation runs into a

61

problem as a stovepipe hat is pretty hard to mistake for anything else, even at night.

As it turns out, the "Haunt Masters Club," a Southern parapsychological research and investigation team, conducted their own research into the legend some years ago and reported that there is no written record of this person or this death ever occurring as the story tells. They also suggest that the story of a two-headed ghost may have derived from an entry in *The Tennessee Encyclopedia of History and Culture* by Carroll Van West that tells of a man who was killed by the Chickamauga Tribe in July of 1776 (as in the month of the very first Independence Day, which might account as a source for why the event took place on the Fourth of July) by scalping. It's quite a loose connection, even by folklore standards, but when it comes to ghost legends in the South, anything is possible.

All the same, the story of the Double-Headed Hitchhiker persists even in the face of this revelatory evidence and is one of *six* purported ghost entities looking for the next gullible motorist to pull over for them on Gap Creek Road, some that may be more aggressive than others.

If you didn't have a good reason to avoid hitchhikers in the South, you do now.

* * * * *

There is an interesting reversal in how ghost lore seems to apply on the streets and highways of the South. With houses, forts, cities, ships, schools, churches, etc., the older it is, the better chance it may be haunted. We hear stories of apparitions who look like they just walked out of 1782 or 1896 more often than someone who came from a year we would remember. This would make sense as those structures have been around long enough to absorb more spiritual residue from those who died onsite, but those who come back to haunt the roads are relatively new. There are many, many more stories of those who died in the last fifty to eighty years returning from their improvised graves and using the automobile as their preferred eidolic vehicle than any other kind on the highways.

Ghosts that use cars to do their immortal bidding are a dime a dozen, but what about a **Phantom Horse-Drawn Wagon** still driving down its old street? That would be considerably rarer and Hilton Head, South Carolina, is where one can be found.

Before it became one of the more famous resorts in the American South, Hilton Head began its history long before much of the rest of the country. 1521 was the year Spanish explorer Francisco Gordillo first made contact with the Native Americans that were living on the island, and by 1600, it became property of the English monarchy. The name itself comes from Captain William Hilton, a "lord proprietor" who had been granted land in the Americas by King Charles II and came to the island from Barbados as a representative to the other lord proprietors. He liked this little island, this "head" of Port Royal Sound, so much that he christened it after himself – "Hilton's Head."

Just over one-hundred years later, in 1776, a sea captain by the name of John Stoney came to purchase one-thousand acres of the island and named it Braddock's Point. In 1793, he began construction for a property that would later become the manor house for the Stoney Plantation, and then the Baynard Plantation by 1840 when John subsequently lost ownership of the house and property to William Eddings Baynard... in a game of poker. Baynard was a man of considerable success already – he owned two lucrative plantations on Edisto Island north of Hilton Head before he even sat down to play the cards, and with three plantations under his management, he was able to introduce Sea Island Cotton to Hilton Head with the same level of prosperity and continued his fortune with it.

But in 1849, his luck ran out, and he died of yellow fever before he even turned fifty years old. He was buried in an above-ground mausoleum in the cemetery of the plantation church. As the Civil War broke out, the widowed Baynard family was forced to flee when Union soldiers made their way to the South Carolina islands in 1861, and turned the Baynard plantation into a headquarters that they used until the war had ended in 1865. Then, at some point between that and the mansion burning down in late 1867 (possibly by former soldiers loyal to the Confederacy), the property was raided by looters who got it into their heads there was treasure hidden in Baynard's mausoleum. Not only did they defile his final resting place by breaking in, the thieves were so determined not to leave their macabre heist empty-handed, that they stole his *body*. By 1868, there was little left to the plantation but ash and a perverse reminder of how hard everything had fallen.

No one knows whatever happened to William Baynard's remains, but it can be inferred that he did not take the calamitous demise of Baynard Plantation well. According to legend, he personifies his eternal lament for their shared ruin in the form of a black, horse-drawn wagon that he rides in the moonlight from the old plantation site through the length of Highway 278 to the Baynard family mausoleum. If that wasn't morbid enough, the legend also states that he is followed by an entire *funeral procession* of the servants, maids and workers that used to work for him, each one as existentially destroyed by the past as he is.

Although that conclusion of the story of William Baynard makes it seem like he wants to replay his own pity party over and over again for all to see, some versions of the legend go further and suggest that he's actually trying to find his missing body, and the servants and additional funeral coaches are there to help him transport whatever he finds of his remains to the family mausoleum to be buried properly. In this version of the story, it is said that this route takes him to a number of plantations and that he stops at each one to look for his body, but, for some reason, he only gets as far as the gates where he stops, stares out onto the property, and then returns to his coach for the next stop.

As it looks quite a bit like the ghostly entourage of William Baynard are simply residual spirits fated to replay the same procession for as long as the future holds, it does bring to mind some good questions: why would William look for his body at the other plantations in Hilton Head and why would he only go as far as the gates if he can go down an entire highway? Was something else going on behind the failed break-in at the former church cemetery or what would motivate him to act in such a strange way?

Well, until William finds what he's looking for, if you happen to see a Black Horse-Driven Wagon on Highway 278 in Hilton Head, give ample room so he can get where he needs to go and be where he needs to be. The roads aren't just for the living, you know!

Creatures of the Night

Earlier in this book, we looked at five categories where most legends in ghost lore fall into, but these categories fail to capture a large section of supernatural beings that have been said to (or you have been warned that) exist in the darkest regions of South, appearing intermittingly in local histories to random, unsuspecting people who survive the encounter with many questions to ask and quite a story to tell. Unlike ghosts and demons, though, these beings are so unique that they exist in categories all their own, and may or may not be demonic, evil, otherworldly, or even alive and corporeal. They may be patchworks of any of those elements or something else entirely, but the one thing we can count on from them is that they scare us as much as any ghost or demon lurking out in the woods.

These creatures have all the potential to make our flesh crawl more than any being we have ever heard of – a ghost at least resembles a formerly living person and a demon, particularly one with a name like **Beelzebub** or **Amon**, could possibly be researched in the bible or another holy scripture, and there, at least, is a modicum of personal reference for a person to rely on. If a little green creature that looks and sounds like nothing on Earth comes to your door, attacks you, and then surrounds your house with an army of their friends and family, what are you supposed to think? What do you rely on there? Folklore thrives on experience with the unknown and therefore these creatures thrive in folklore, particularly in the South where thousands of hiding places exist just outside the safety of the campfire or tree house.

Creature-based stories also have an interesting advantage to ghost-based legends in that we have plenty of proof that weird and unbelievable beings roam every inch of the planet, and, therefore, have a slightly higher chance of being true – consider the duck-billed platypus: an aquatic, poisonous mammal that can *lay eggs*, the golden orb spider that can grow large enough to eat *a snake*, or the deep-ocean dwelling giant squid that used to exist only as a nautical fairytale itself until a French dispatch steamer discovered and tried to retrieve one in 1861, securing enough of the creature's flesh to set the precedent that some monsters *really do exist* in the world.

And while the monsters in this chapter will likely never receive that kind of scientific accolade due to their wildly fantastic properties and purported abilities (it's hard to deliver a body to science if that body can turn into mist, for example), if we have learned anything in the thousands of years that we have been discovering new plants, animals, lands and planets, it's that "life is stranger than fiction." If one fairytale can prove to be true, if at least to less exaggerated proportions, then who knows which one of these creatures will be fully discovered and documented next?

The answer may surprise and terrify us.

* * * * *

Between two Jacksonvilles, in North Carolina and Florida respectively, and in cities like Savannah, Georgia, exists the descendents of the Gullah African Americans of the South Carolina lowlands. The "Gullah" name may not immediately ring a bell to many today, but if you remember the story of **Br'er Rabbit** from Uncle Remus, or ever had fried okra, or ever sang the song "Kumbaya" with your church, you have already been introduced to elements of the Gullah culture. Gullah continues to flourish with great pride in the coastal South nearly five centuries after the West Africans were forced onto the Carolina shores as part of the plantation slave trade. They came to represent the common bloodline of the slave labor force for rice and cotton plantations with their strong bodies and the generations-old knowledge of farming that they brought from their homeland. When the Civil War swept over the country, the plantation owners on the Sea Islands fled their properties, leaving the Gullah with their first taste of freedom in over three-hundred years. In the 1940s, their descendents came to dominate the hospitality industries in their respective states and continue to survive and thrive today as a major pillar of the coastal communities in the South.

No book on Southern folklore is complete without talking about the Gullah culture and the tales that they adapted from their roots in Africa to their surroundings and experiences here in America. The foundation it serves for Southern folklore as a whole cannot be understated, with dozens of well-known stories featuring tricksters, fables, and, yes, ghosts and demons, and their contribution to regional ghost lore may be one of the most frightening monsters ever conceived on American soil – the **Boo Hag**.

Even a description of the Boo Hag takes some effort to successfully imagine, as it is described as a vampire, witch, shape-shifter and skinless terror all at once, with a red bodily color of naked muscles and bones, an ability to drain the life force out of a living person by sucking in their sleeping breath (interestingly referred to as "riding" a person) and an uncompromising obsession with trying to steal their victims' skin. It is said that if a Boo Hag is after you, all they have to do is enter your house through a small crack from the outside, or any tiny entry device they can find, and wait until you're asleep

69

so they can drain you. Once drained, you're left in a deep sleep marred by dreams and an almost lifeless state of being.

And the worst part? They go to painstaking measures to make sure they drain as much out of you before you die and then leave you just barely alive so they can keep feeding off of your life force for days on end. After a while, you *wish* it were just an evil spirit or demon haunting your house.

Somewhat amusingly, the legend of the Boo Hag was actually spread through the Gullah culture and the Southern states as a tale against stranger danger – be careful what company you keep, otherwise you might find yourself sharing a bed with a shape-shifting evil that wants to siphon the air right out of your body and then strip you of your skin if you dare to fight back (if that isn't effective as a deterrent, nothing is).

The traditional story goes that a young man in the Gullah South was getting old enough to have a wife of his own, but just could not find a woman who would make it all the way to the altar with him. He often shared his frustrations with his father, who owned a grocery store, and one day the father came into contact with a woman from the swamp that had a daughter who was also looking for a mate. They had their children meet at the next town dance and the attraction was instantaneous – in fact, they had so much fun that by sunrise, they wanted to get *married*, and by evening, they were.

But in the few days following the impulsive nuptials, an odd pattern was emerging out of the new bride. During the daytime, she cooked and cleaned the house as a good wife should, but during the night, she refused to go to bed until just before it was dawn, and when she did finally get under the covers with him, she was noticeably hot and sweaty. When pressed for a reason behind this strange habit, she responded with fire from her eyes and poison from her tongue. The man became so worried that he contacted the local "conjure woman," a shaman of sorts, and she told him to pretend to go to asleep as he usually did, and then spy on her nocturnal activities.

The man did as he was told the next night and secretly watched in horror as his beautiful bride stripped off her skin with a spinning wheel up in the attic, as if it were thread, and then flew out into the city from the top story window looking like a naked corpse. The unbelievable sight stirred the man from head to toe and he spent the rest of the night in bed, shaken, and unable to go to sleep with that image burned in his mind. It only became more uncomfortable for him when she returned in the morning as she always did, as if nothing had happened, with the beautiful bride's skin on her face and body that he last saw in a *spool* upstairs. He knew he had to do something about this, and fast.

The next chance he got, the man returned to the conjure woman and told her what he saw. She knew immediately it was a Boo Hag and spared few words explaining to him what one was and how to get rid of it. The conjure woman told the man to paint the frames of each door and window blue, as the Boo Hag cannot cross that color (for some reason), and to patch up any hole outside the house that she could squeeze in (some versions of the story also mention putting salt and pepper on the skin to irritate her). If she could not get back to her skin before daybreak, she would die as the sunlight would burn her alive in a matter of minutes.

At first, the man was highly hesitant to do such a thing, as it meant an unwelcome return to a reluctant bachelorhood, but he also knew that any day now, he could be the next item on her menu... so when she left again that night, he went to work painting all the frames and patching all the cracks and holes he could find. Daybreak came and, sure enough, she could not enter the house again. She flew around the house desperately looking for a way in, but she could not get back to her skin in time and burst into flames on his doorstep.

Legends of Boo Hags are steeped with the old-time Southern superstitions that held home remedies for keeping them away – keeping a fork under the pillow, laying a broom on the floor, which was said to distract them as they could not resist counting the straws, and keeping a loaded gun at the nightstand with the barrel aimed at the foot of the bed, as Boo Hags hate the smell of gunpowder (or to make them think twice about riding tonight). For those familiar with all the folklore of vampires from across the world, much of this comes off very similar to the famous Wallachian race of bloodsuckers, who also fell victim the rays of the sun, flew in the form of a bat, and could be repelled by garlic or anything resembling a cross. They, however, could not walk in the daytime no matter whose skin they had.

So if a Boo Hag is essentially a vampire that *can* walk in the daytime, you can imagine how horrifying it would be to find yourself suddenly married to one. As the descendents of the Gullah people today are still very tight-knit along the Southern coasts and islands, it seems they took this lesson to heart, learned how to keep good company with one another and kept stories like these alive for new generations to understand the value of their wisdom. The Gullah are far from the first people to use folklore to educate, but arguably the best at it here in the South.

* * * * *

From South Carolina, we travel to its northern brother to find a town called Murphy, in Cherokee County. The site of Murphy is no stranger to stories and legends of bizarre creatures, as they have been said to exist there since the days of the Cherokee Native Americans when they referred to it as

Tlanusi-yi – the home of the giant leech **Tlanusi** that was said to live in the Hiwassee River near Murphy. Of the modern folklore, there are stories of clocks that growl at you, microwaves that cook without aid of electricity and several more, almost routine, stories of haunts you can find in most towns, but one house is said to have them all beat with a very strange visitor you can only find in Murphy: **The House Of The Gnome**.

Probably the best account of this elusive creature was a story said to take place in the 1950s when a family with two boys moved into a three-story house that, previous to their entry, had no history of abnormal activity. Indeed, once it began, it began slowly... waiting almost a month for the family to get settled in their new house before the two boys started hearing strange laughter coming from the hallways. Then, in the following weeks, there were loud knocks on their bedroom doors demanding their attention, yet the hallways would always be empty when they went to see who was keeping them awake. Then there were soft footsteps and shuffling heard on the staircase and third floor of the house. The boys went to their parents and told them all about the sounds they were hearing. The parents, as most usually do, laughed and reassured them that there wasn't anything weird going on in the house, instead that it was only making the same noises every other house in the country makes on a regular basis.

It was true, the boys had next to nothing to go on but noises, and there wasn't any history of death, murder or ritual in the house, so it couldn't be haunted. Yet the noises continued unabated. *Something* was in that house, but what?

Then one day, one of the boys was listening to a record player in his room when his brother and a visiting friend came tearing in, hyperventilating, saying they found the creature that had been making those noises and it was in the bathroom. He laughed at the pair and humored them as he made his way to

73

the bathroom. He stopped laughing, however, when he opened the door and found a small humanoid figure, barely over 2 ft. tall, with a twisted face and arms so long they couldn't be real, staring and laughing right back at him. It bolted out between his legs and disappeared in one of its many hiding places.

From there on, the "Gnome," as they called it for lack of a better word, would turn up at the oddest of times throughout the months and always scamper away before anyone could get their hands on it. They heard his little laughter in the hallways and his constant dashing and jumping in the walls and rooms they couldn't see it in. Finally, when their father finally saw it for himself in the master bedroom, he decided enough was enough and the family moved out one week later.

Decades later, the house was said to be cursed by this gnome, or whatever it was, as no one would stay in it long enough to find out what the beast really was... and what it wanted.

Not much more of this creature seems to be known, but there is a similar legend also coming out of Murphy, North Carolina that ties back in with the Native Americans that lived there before it was settled. The Cherokee used to tell stories of a race of small, bearded, humanoid men with pale skin they called **The Moon-Eyed People**, because they were nocturnal as the sunlight was too bright for their eyes. The Moon-Eyed people also came from Hiwassee before it was Murphy, and they were often in conflict with the Native Americans until a major skirmish with either the Creek or the Cherokee tribes forced them to retreat from their homeland up into the mountains. They dug themselves into the caverns and rock and presumably still survive there today with mounds and small walls built throughout the Southern Appalachians.

Is there a connection between the two legends? Could this gnome be some sort of otherworldly "answer" to the persecution of the Moon-Eyed People? It *is* just a bit too coincidental that two different legends about such similar beings would exist in one town, but as there are further tales of little people and monstrous versions thereof existing throughout the state of North Carolina, there may be a whole untapped reservoir of history, folklore and crypto-anthropology/zoology that we're missing out on.

Maybe instead of looking back at history for answers to our mysteries, we should start looking down?

* * * * *

Speaking of tiny little creatures with long arms, we venture west of North Carolina to Tennessee where there was, or still might be, a widespread belief among children in an even more exaggerated and far more humorous gremlin called **Squeezer**.

The Squeezer legend belongs to an extended family of "boogeyman" tales – stories of unspeakable evils that prey on children from the closet, underneath the bed, or the darkest corner of the room that their nightmares always spring from. Nearly everyone remembers going through this phase in their lifetime with some evil beast that existed in the bedtime ritual without question, no matter how outlandish it was described to be, and Squeezer fits that model to a tee. Being only 3-4 in. tall, about the size of a can of soda, it somehow has arms that are long enough to wrap around a person several times over, with large muscles in those arms to squeeze anything it has in its grasp until they breathe their last breath. Furthermore, it can apparently speak English, hold an intelligent conversation, and even be noticeably hurt and sensitive if you do not respect him as a boogeyman, which is more of a job title for him than anything.

Just what kind of a creature is this, anyway? How would something like that even be able to move with such imbalanced proportions, much less be able to terrorize and render harm on someone?

I first came across this legend in the book *More Haunted Tennessee* by Charles Edwin Price about seven years ago and he tells the story of a twelve-year-old girl named Jeannie and a friend who was staying over for the night. After the lights went out, a pair of long, bony hands came up over the foot of the bed and reached toward Jeannie, but instead of cowering in fear as she saw them approach, she instead grabbed a baseball bat that was nearby and repeatedly bashed the little devil with it.

To her surprise, the monster actually pleaded for her to stop. When she did to listen to what it had to say, Squeezer, as it introduced itself to Jeannie, tried to put up another menacing front that was quickly shot back down as the two girls started mocking his name and absurd body structure. Squeezer then became vocally disappointed that these two girls were not afraid of him and told them that they needed to be scared so he could do his job right. The girls only laughed harder at him, and his patience proved even shorter than his stature when he lunged forth to squeeze them anyway.

Jeannie and her friend fought back and put up a good struggle against the pint-sized puck until Jeannie's father came in and told them to quit horsing around. Little Squeezer, though, was gone by then, and the girls went back to bed.

Very soon after the light went out, though, a set of bony hands came up over foot of the bed again. Jeannie, almost casually, reached for the bat to give Squeezer another good thrashing... when *another* set of hands reached up onto the bed alongside it. Then another, and another, and another still.

Now Jeannie had a good reason to be genuinely afraid – Squeezer didn't leave so he wouldn't get caught... he only went for *backup*.

By now, we have a pretty good idea what the point of this story is, not all ghosts and monsters have to be dripping with blood and leaving a body count just to tell a good story. There are actually quite a few tales of supernatural beings that are far from the dark, sad and gruesome blights we usually hear about, some can be quite lighthearted and even beneficial – I even remember hearing of one ghost out in the world somewhere that would make a shower of money rain from the ceiling to help its hosts pay off a financial crisis.

* * * * *

Another mythical beast from Tennessee that seems to inspire as much mirth as it does mayhem is the famous **Wampus Cat**, a legendary cougar/cat with six legs (and possibly a spiked ball on its tail) that is said to be the tragic spirit of a Native American woman. This curious maiden, for whatever reason, decided to dress in cougar skins so she could spy on the men of her tribe while they were out in the fields. It is not known why she was spying on them, but the medicine man was still not too pleased when he found her out there and, as a major consequence for a minor offense, immediately placed a curse on her that would keep her trapped in the form of an enchanted cat, seemingly for all eternity.

She was said to haunt the Cades Cove area of Blount County in East Tennessee, and many hunting parties of the early 20th century in that area went out looking for her when she was sighted... at least that's what the men all told their families. In reality, they were just looking for an excuse to get away from their near-puritan families and have a moonshine party in the basement of the local grocery store. The image of the Wampus Cat today still inspires festivity as the sports mascot of at least six schools in the U.S.

The power of folklore can touch and shape our society in very significant ways – stories can make us feel heartache from hundreds of years ago, scare us smart or silly, educate us with the wisdom of generations in just a few minutes' time, or even give us an excellent opportunity to put down our fears and have a good time with the company of our fellow men.

After all, if the stories can't be fun once in a while, what's the point in telling them?

* * * * *

Before we leave Tennessee, there is one more creature rumored to be roaming the state at night that, unlike The Wampus Cat and Squeezer, is most certainly *not* something you want to joke around with.

In Dickson County, of West Tennessee, there is a small town by the name of White Bluff. It is named after the many white-colored bluffs against Turnbull Creek, and served as the site for Fort White Bluffs in 1806 before the town was formally incorporated in 1869. The town is very attenuated and not known for much more than being the second largest city in Dickson County, the education and literacy efforts of Jeannie Woodworth in the early 20th century, and the near 50% population growth between 2000 and 2010. It's the kind of town you want to visit when you want to get some genuine peace and quiet in the South.

But on some nights, it is said, that peace and quiet is ironically shattered by a sinister, ferocious entity that shrieks at an ear-splitting volume, warning you to get out of the area as fast as you can. White Bluff is known for one other thing – the legend of **The White Screamer**.

To call this thing a "beast" barely does the word justice, as the White Screamer is a fearsome fiend that appears either in the form of a pure white behemoth with four legs, or as a cloud of mist that gets its terrifying name from the long, pitch-bending, bloodcurdling howl it will make incessantly throughout the night. It may have human hands and is said to burn the grass where it treads, even in mist form. Some have suggested the White Screamer is a form of a "banshee," a sort of spirit of Irish and Welsh origin that is also known to wail stretched, evil notes when someone nearby was going to die. Others have said the White Screamer is the evil spirit of an unknown person who was murdered more than a century ago in White Bluff. Some even go as far as to claim the White Screamer is an escaped zoo animal that continues to haunt the woods of the area even today.

The first account of the White Screamer is the story of a young man in the 1920s that came to have a family of his own, a wife and seven children, and built a large house out in the hollow where he could raise all of his children up. Not long after he finished the house, he started hearing a very loud and very disturbing symphony of screams nearby that made it impossible to sleep. This happened *every single night* after he had moved into the house, and finally, one night, the man decided enough was enough. After everyone else went to bed, he took his shotgun, loaded it up, and went on a midnight hunt. Like clockwork, whatever was making this noise had started up once again; that night he swore that he was going to find it and shut it up for good.

But the hunt proved frustrating. He searched for hours but could not find the source of this awful sound. He came to a hill and decided to climb it to see if he could spot his prey at a distance, but then there was a new screaming sound cutting through the night air... and it was coming from his house. The man hurried home as fast as he could but it was too late. He found his family in pieces, scattered across the house with ashen steps burned into the floor. That story ends there, but one only has to imagine what the aftermath for that man must have been.

Another account took place years later as a hunter in the area killed a deer and took it back to his house to be dressed.

He had his backyard set up for skinning and cleaning, and when he was done, he put the leftover parts in an outdoor bathtub he had set aside for that purpose.

Later that night, as he was out on the porch playing his guitar, he suddenly became aware that something just wasn't right outside – there was dead silence, without a single croaking frog or cricket to be heard. Then his two hound dogs, which had somehow gotten out, came running to him from the other side of the house. He looked from the direction they had come from and there it was... the White Screamer in all its horrible glory, heading right for him.

He was barely able to escape inside the house, and he had to hold the front door to keep the monster from getting in. It pushed hard, screamed even harder and scratched up the wood of the door to get in, but the hunter, with all his might, was still able to (barely) defend his home. The creature finally relented after a long struggle and made its way to the other side of the house. The hunter used the break to retrieve his rifle, and waited for it to try to come in through the back so that he could shoot it.

He waited for several minutes, then several hours, and before he knew it, the sun was rising. He hadn't seen or heard the Screamer since it went around the back, and with great caution, the hunter decided to see what was going on. He opened the back door to find... nothing. The Screamer had gone with the sunlight, and when the hunter went towards the bathtub that had the deer entrails, he found they were also gone without a single ounce of carcass left behind.

Finally, some years after that, the third reported encounter with the White Screamer took place at a fishing spot along the Big Turnbull Creek where a wife and her husband were fishing. They had early luck catching a good haul of fish and made their way further down the river to bring in even more. As it started getting dark, they realized they went too far down the riverbank, but they decided to try to get back to the truck before nightfall. While walking back, the wife stumbled along the path and twisted her ankle, and as the husband was helping her up, he noticed something was following them – although he couldn't see it.

When he heard it getting closer, the man suddenly dropped both the fish and the rods and led his wife down into the water so that they could see what was following them. They just barely got far enough away before a white gargantuan stepped out of the shadows and fed on their catch. The couple couldn't believe their eyes at the sight of this thing, and when it had finished eating, it picked up their fishing rods with its human-like hands and appeared to be studying them. Suddenly, it seemed to detect their scent, and started looking around for whoever left the fish.

While they were a safe distance from the White Screamer, they could not get to their truck with the creature on the banks in front of them. The husband broke away from his wife and tried several tactics to lure it away so she could get to the truck and start it up for a quick getaway, but all he managed to do was lure it on a bank right next to their vehicle. This almost closed that window of opportunity and escape. Now the Screamer was perfectly aware that the both of them were there, and all they could do was run for their lives while it chased them. At that point, there was one final option left – an old, abandoned farmhouse near that bank where they might at least have solid walls to protect them from their pursuer.

With great difficulty, they made it to the house safe and sound, but the Screamer was so close to catching them that the only way they could close the farmhouse door was to slam it in the monster's face. They barricaded the door with their bodies and listened as it circled the house, blaring its horrible, screeching siren all night until they nearly went insane from the noise.

81

Finally, as day broke, the creature again became oddly silent. The husband peered outside and found no trace of it anywhere near them. As soon as the coast was clear, they raced to the truck, desperate to leave this place and never come back, only to find their rods and reels in the truck bed. For some reason, at some point during the night, the Screamer decided to return their fishing equipment to them.

What a mysterious monster indeed. Next to the Bell Witch, I don't think there is a more dangerous and harrowing evil in the state of Tennessee. We can take some solace in the fact that some of these stories are so unbelievable that they couldn't possibly have happened in a town as quiet as White Bluff, but if you ever find yourself driving through there one night, you might want to bring some raw meat and a pair of earplugs just in case.

* * * * *

As states go here in the U.S., Kentucky is not the first place one might assume is a hotbed for stories of cryptids and bizarre creatures, but even the least skeptical person on the subject might balk at some of the reports that come out of the Bluegrass State. Besides being the homeland of the **Goat Man** of Pope Lick Tresle, the **Lizard Man** in Trimble County, and even **Bigfoot** (which had its share of sightings in the state starting in the 1960s and 1970s), Kentucky is also well-known for dozens of UFO and extraterrestrial sightings reported throughout the more recent decades, with the story of **The Kelly-Hopkinsville Goblins** being one of the earliest and creepiest of those encounters in the South.

Depending on whom you might ask, stories of aliens and spacecrafts run either parallel or perpendicular to ghosts, demons, and monsters in the realm of paranormal study. These creatures are not magic or supernatural (in theory, at least), they're just simply different life forms from an unknown mortal environment, same as any other life forms that science could discover and quantity. They may or may not be evil according to our standards, and could possess recognizable benevolence or even greater intelligence than we do (they would actually need to in order to travel from planet to planet, a feat we have yet to master). But like the ghosts and demons of our planet, they represent a great mystery to the human condition and the confirmation of their existence would revolutionize our way of life. Even those who thumb their nose at supernatural entities on the basis of science may readily admit extraterrestrial life forms have a higher chance of existing somewhere in the universe. They wouldn't be much different than some of the strange creatures you can find on Earth, so why would they frighten us as much as a ghost or demon?

At least part of *that* answer starts back in 1955 near Hopkinsville of Christian County, Kentucky, a scant eight years after the first reported sighting of nine flying objects that could not be identified over Mount Rainier in the state of Washington, and only seven years after the famous **Roswell Incident** of New Mexico. UFO history was quite young at that time, and yet the phenomenon was exploding all over the country with twelve-*thousand* cases reported between 1952 and 1969. To take this into account alongside the still very rural, rugged, and arguably somewhat primitive nature of the South at that time and what happened on the night of August 21st of that year becomes understandably bone-chilling.

That night, in a farmhouse between Kelly and Hopkinsville, a family of eleven by the name of Sutton was sitting down to supper when a family friend named Billy Taylor, who had been visiting and staying for the meal, went outside to draw some water from the well. He just happened to look up as he walked out to the well and saw a flying circular object zoom across the sky into the woods not far away. Billy rushed inside to tell everyone what he had seen, but, predictably, no one took him seriously... at first.

Suddenly, the family dogs started barking at the door. Billy and Lucky Sutton each grabbed a gun and prepared themselves to see what was out front. They barely had to open the door when they saw a small, green figure about three feet tall, come out of the shadows towards them with its hands up. A wave of panic at the sight of this thing came over the two men and they immediately opened fire, barraging the visitor with a hail of bullets. The creature was so amazingly agile that it managed to avoid being shot at point blank range and then retreated back to the woods. Billy and Lucky chose not to pursue it and went back inside the farmhouse.

It was only a few minutes later when they saw it again – this time it had a large, green head that was peering into their house from the window. Guns still at their sides, they fired at it from inside the house and this time was at least able to hit it, but when they went outside to see if it was dead, an enormous claw came from the roof behind them and grabbed onto Billy's head.

Billy managed to tear himself away from the monster and again they escaped back into the house. Now that the whole family saw what was going on, everyone worked fast to barricade the doors and windows. During the rush, the family all witnessed more of the same creatures appearing around the house, circling the building and seemingly preparing for a massive assault. Other family members picked up their guns and shot at the creatures through the windows. One of the goblins was reportedly hit and was said to have glowed for a few seconds on the ground before scampering off on all fours where it couldn't be seen. The battle lasted for almost four hours when the family decided to make a break for the police station and get help. They broke through the alien invasion, got into their cars and safely made it to the station. The invaders did not follow.

Surprisingly, the deputy sheriff did not dismiss their crazy story and obliged to help them out. He and several officers armed themselves and prepared to do battle with the green horde, but when they got to the farmhouse, there was nothing there. The only evidence of the battle was the broken glass of the windows.

The officers searched until 2:20AM and then left rather irritated by the event, but only seconds after the last police car vacated the property, another series of green heads popped back into the windows and the battle was back on. This time, the invasion raged on until it was dawn when the strange gremlin-looking things finally opted to retreat. This time, they left for good.

The Sutton family contacted the police again, and the police contacted the Air Force, starting off a chain reaction of go-nowhere investigations and a media circus that descended on the family as part of the growing public fascination and hysteria with extraterrestrials. Each Sutton was interviewed multiple times by police, news reporters, authors and other interested parties, and the story each interviewee received always remained the same. Interestingly, while patronizing "theories" of escaped circus monkeys and mass alcoholism (which would not explain how eleven drunk people were all hallucinating the same thing) came forth from dissenters in town and across the country, people who were miles and miles away at the time and yet could still explain what happened better than those who were there, no evidence of a hoax was ever recovered at any time around the property.

The story of the events survived the test of time where the "rational explanations" did not. To this day, and to the experts who study and dispute claims of UFO encounters, the Kelly-Hopkinsville Goblins case is considered to be an authentic case of an extraterrestrial attack, and an unnerving reminder that not every monster in folklore proves to be just a fairytale.

Where the Dead Live

One of the most mysterious aspects of the subject of ghosts seems to revolve around their attachment to certain places and objects. If it is true that some, if not all, previously living people retain a consciousness similar to what they had before they died and are no longer bound by the physical limits of the body, then why would they spend hundreds of years existentially locked inside a moldy old house that's crumbling from the roof down? Why wouldn't they finally explore the entirety of the world or go further out into the universe now that they can?

Perhaps the transition from vessel to entity simply changes the limitations of existence instead of removing them. As anyone who knows more than a few ghost stories can reason, a majority of hauntings in folklore throughout the world take place inside a building or landmark instead of out in the open. Ghosts and evil entities are extremely territorial, and even the most vicious demonic presence seems to prefer planting its infernal roots down in a concentrated area instead of traveling from place to place looking for new victims. An entity may remain at its chosen location for hundreds of years or more until it is either exorcised or the building it haunts simply burns to the ground. Its level of protectiveness for that area will highly vary.

There are a few strong hypotheses for their attachments – the first being that spirits, highly emotional by nature, refuse to leave an area that they once called home or found genuine happiness in. Fear of the unknown does not necessarily need to be excluded only to the living, and if you were faced with the most uncertain future of all, would you not want to stay somewhere that was familiar to you before? There are no rules now, why wouldn't you want to stay at your favorite museum or bar as long as you truly wanted?

Another hypothesis states that ghosts have unfinished business and cannot accept that they are dead when they had so much else to do. Many ghost stories feature lives that were cut short in their prime, just before their wedding, or when they were guilty of a grave injustice of which they never redeemed themselves. Others were cut down by a careless mistake, unpredictable accident, or an unfair misfortune they could not avoid suffering no matter what. Death under tragic circumstances has a high potency for transforming souls into spirits according to ghost lore, and the dead may angrily exile themselves back to their former houses and refuse to share it others, defending their property so they can wallow in their almighty depression indefinitely. Worse still, some ghosts may not even *know* they're dead and somehow remain able to act and interact as they used to without noticing the difference.

It really does make one wonder what it was about life that made these consciousnesses yearn so deeply for it – life many hundreds of years ago in the South was not fun at all. You worked from sunup to sundown almost every day from early childhood to very old age, for no other reason than to survive another year, and then do it all again. You were easily susceptible to diseases that could wipe you out slowly and painfully before you even knew you had it, and you had to have a great number of children just because you knew only a few of them would live to be twelve years old. Everything was harder than it needed to be and help might be nowhere in sight. If you had dark skin, you basically had no chance to live your own life even under those circumstances. One would think they couldn't wait to die, for what else is there to be attached to?

The final major hypothesis for ghosts haunting a specified place, called the "Stone Tape theory," helps answer this by suggesting that spirits aren't consciousness at all. According to this theory, spirits are just residual energy from a person that was left imprinted from their lives after a dramatic scene (like one's own murder, for example) released it into the atmosphere, and now replays the scene at certain time intervals. Although there are quite a few hauntings that certainly do this, it does not apply to a much greater variety of ghosts out in the world and begs the question of why other dramatic scenes do not regularly replay in rooms or houses.

Every building has its secrets, and if walls could talk, they would definitely scream. We may never know the answers to these questions until we join the dead and remain with them for many a year ourselves, but at least we can find some clues to how the science of spirits might work in the meantime, and in the South, we can find some truly hair-raising examples of that science that remind us of why we fear the dead in the first place.

Let's begin this journey in South Carolina at a most unusual inn...

* * * * *

Haunted hotels are a dime a dozen here in the South. Anywhere from a secluded Bed and Breakfast to the Best Western down the street may have something there, depending on the veracity of local lore, but few accommodations in our corner of the country are said to be haunted with *pirate* ghosts and departed gentlemen. **The Battery Carriage House Inn** of Charleston, South Carolina is one of those very few.

If legends are to be believed, Charleston is already stuffed to the gills with spirits wandering freely throughout the city, so it takes more than a little bit of notoriety for a building to win the title of "Charleston's Most Haunted Inn" year after year. Many first-hand accounts have come out of the Battery Carriage House and continue to do so as the hotel proudly remains in business to this day. They even list the rooms reported to be haunted *on their own website.*

Well before all that was established folklore in Charleston, the Battery Carriage House was property that had been purchased in 1843 by wealthy commercial agent Samuel N. Stevens for a sum of $4,500. He apparently lived in the building and renovated it until 1859 when he sold it to John Blacklock, who soon abandoned the house out of the fear of the Civil War advancing down on South Carolina. He still owned the house and sold it in 1870 to Colonel Richard Lathers of the Union, who went on to renovate it further after its damage during the war. Despite his efforts to fit in and use his new property to bring peace between the North and South by inviting leaders from both sides to break bread with each other, Lathers was not well liked in Charleston, and it soon found yet another new owner with phosphate mining business man Andrew Simonds. His descendant, Drayton Hastie, now owns the property and, according to the history of the property as written on the website, it seems to have had a reasonably happy history with no murders or unusually tragic deaths occurring inside the hotel.

So what exactly makes this the most haunted inn in Charleston?

The answer to that seems to be as puzzling to the staff as it is to anyone else. It is said that many small abnormalities take place all throughout the property – window shutters opening and closing by themselves, glowing lights, footsteps, being watched by those that can't be watched back... standard features of a hotel haunting that do not seem to have easily identifiable sources.

Then there are three hotel rooms that are said to have concentrated activities, as reported, again, by the hotel itself. Room #3 seems to have once been either a portal or a meeting site for many random spirits to gather in, as one couple found out. At an undisclosed time, a man and his wife were sleeping in the room when the man's cell phone started blinking and making noise the first night they were staying. Stirring from their sleep, they remembered the phone had been turned off and they were not able to get a phone signal in the room when it was on. Soon after that, something started illuminating from the bathroom while the faucet began to release water on its own, and the night ended with the both of them watching shapes and energies float in and around the room presumably until morning or until they fell asleep. On the second night (yes, they were brave enough to stay a *second* night), the activity started up again with the glowing form appearing in the sitting room and the other shapes and energies joining it. Again, the brave couple simply stuck it out through the night. Sometime later, by some wild stroke of luck, they ran into another guest at the hotel, named Susan, who was clairvoyant and offered to help them restore some order in their room. Susan went with them to Room #3 and found there really was an enormous spiritual presence there. She commanded the spirits to leave and the couple reportedly had a much more peaceful night. This account ends on that note and it appears that that room is no longer haunted, but whatever the entities were, or why a medium with that kind of power would only exorcise one room are different mysteries altogether.

I would suppose one reason for that is that a more famous haunt of the hotel is known affectionately as the "Gentleman

Ghost" of Room #10. He is not a threatening spirit in the least, though his general activity may be quite scary all the same to the women who stay there. It is said the Gentleman Ghost has a habit of wanting to crawl into bed with any woman who sleeps alone in Room #10, and if the woman protests or screams (who wouldn't?) the entity will simply exit the bed, go back to his business through an entertainment unit that used to be the original door to the room, and not bother the lady any further. I'm not sure how this ghost qualifies as a gentleman for that habit, nor was I able to find out what happens if someone *does* share the bed with him, but he seems to carry a reasonably pleasant presence all the same and is even said to smell like fresh soap (somehow).

But the entity haunting Room #8 is no hygienic cavalier, he's a headless torso wearing clothes from centuries past that appears on the bedside to any guest unfortunate enough to wake up and see him. It is said that this ghost has a menacing personality, rasping and growling at the living without the need of his head, and can even be touched. One man, who stayed in the room in 1993, woke up to find the terrifying shade in front of him on the bedside, reached out to touch the figure and felt the fabric of his overcoat (described to be something like a coarse burlap). The man screamed when the headless torso started growling, but before the entity could do anything harmful, it apparently just vanished before the guest's eyes, leaving him thoroughly shaken by the disturbance and no longer skeptical of the supernatural.

There are two ideas as to who the headless man could be – one is that he was a Civil War soldier who lost everything above his neck in a munitions accident, and the other is that he might be the pirate ghost of Stede Bonnet, "The Gentleman Pirate," from the early 18th century. Stede is said to haunt several places around Charleston already after his appeals for a pardon failed to generate anything but a hanging for piracy.

Apart from the ghost having old clothes, though, there doesn't seem to be any way to properly guess his true identity.

Complicating matters further is a second account reported on the hotel's website – another couple was staying in the room when the wife was awoken by the sounds of the window shutters moving on their own. Suddenly, a shadow moved over the shutters and she went into the bathroom to turn the light on, presumably so she could see what it was that just moved through their room. Later, the husband got up and found there was a frosty-looking face in the mirror that soon disappeared. Whether or not this was a different entity or a strange manifestation of the headless man's identity is just as inexplicable as everything else going on at the Battery Carriage House, but now we start to see how the hotel keeps its title.

One has to wonder if there is more to the history of the inn than the official public version wants to share. The Gentleman Ghost, for example, is said to be the spirit of a college student who jumped off the roof of the building to his death, yet the same management that openly admits to the hotel being haunted does not mention this in their account of the building's history. It is rather unusual that the most haunted inn in Charleston would be clean of the human calamity that typically inducts spirits into the physical world in the first place.

Then again, if their afterlife is as constantly depressing as they sometimes make it out to be, could it be that ghosts just need a vacation sometimes as well?

* * * * *

With a name like **The Moody Brick**, you might get first impressions of a brick house with an air of sorrow and a long, dormant chronicle of tragedy that created the dark, bleak atmosphere surrounding the property today... and you couldn't be more right if you tried. The big, two-story L-shaped relic of the mid-19th century is a landmark in Kyles of Jackson County, Alabama, well-known locally for its historical significance and even better known regionally for being soaked to the cement pores with rumors of ghostly activity.

Giving a house a name like "The Moody Brick" seems to initiate a self-fulfilling prophecy. It is, in fact, named after the Moody family who came to purchase the building and the farmland property in 1872. Brothers Miles, James, and later, John Moody, worked for many years to turn the relatively young site into the Moody Farm and they had their work cut out for them. Heavy cotton planting had rendered the soil virtually impotent and it needed to rest before it could become productive again. Other parts of the farmland were literally burned-out after soldiers from the Union came in the mid-1860s, took over the property, used it as they saw fit, and apparently set fire to the house and surrounding areas when they were done. After that, the house itself corroded and deteriorated for a number of years until it changed hands to the Moody brothers. By 1879, so much progress had been made that a reporter from the *Alabama Herald* devoted more than 800 words of article space on the paper just to describe how much had improved since the brothers began renovating.

Even for a plantation with heavy fire damage and soil exhaustion, seven years of work with competent management is a long time to rejuvenate a property. Just what happened to such a stately-looking place to put it in so much disrepair?

The answer? *Everything.* The house had been steeped in mystery since it was built. There is even significant controversy of *when* the house was built and *by whom*. The earliest known record of transaction for the site seems to have occurred in 1830 when one-hundred-and-sixty acres of land was purchased by a C.B. Hudson from the Huntsville Land Office. Between 1830 and 1855, a builder was commissioned to start construction on a main house for the property which was to be occupied by a Mary Ann Hudson (very likely a descendant of C.B. Hudson) and her husband Carter Overton Harris. As Mary was born in 1817 and had her daughter Pattie Kate in 1841 by Carter Overton, it is likely the house was commissioned for the both of them close to 1840, or at the very least was just land in C.B.'s possession for several years before an architect was sought. The man believed to be the builder was Hiram Higgins, the man who was responsible for designing the old courthouses of Scottsboro and Moulton, Alabama, and the school buildings in Athens and Talladega. The very start of The Moody Brick's history is considerably muddy, and it doesn't get any better for years to come.

The property was an archetypical Southern plantation and it is said that Carter and Mary were archetypical Southern slave owners. Legends abound that the African workers on the farm were routinely brutalized by their supervisors – beaten, bashed, blooded, chained and even murdered in the dungeon-like slaves' quarters beneath the house. The locals, who were aware of what was going on at the plantation, kept their mouths shut to the authorities because slave abuse was simply the norm in those days, but even they secretly confessed among themselves how horrified they were at what was said to be going on over there. Those confessions turned into gossip that formed the basis of the Moody Brick folklore as we know it today (yet somehow still did not reach the ears of the authorities).

Without the authorities intervening, the slaves decided to take the law into their own strong hands and, according to the legend, lead a violent uprising to their supervisors shortly *after* the Civil War ended (which would mean that the African workers were being enslaved there illegally). Each of their brutal masters, except Carter who died in 1860, was slain in the outbreak. They were able to escape the property altogether and for a while it looked like they were finally free... until the Ku Klux Klan got wind of the uprising and took it upon themselves to round up the slaves and hang them from a tree in front of an angry lynch mob at the Moody Brick. While the oral tradition for these accounts are very strong in Alabama, there is no written historical evidence that this deadly uprising and its baleful aftermath ever happened, though at least we have a good first source of the purported haunting.

A second possible source is suggested as the legend further states that the house was used as a Civil War field hospital between 1863 and 1864. Confederate soldiers of the Chattanooga and Chickamauga campaigns were brought into the house in hopes of treating the copious ghastly wounds they had sustained on the battlefield, and many were agonized to death onsite. At this time, the slaves would have still been agonized themselves by their masters, according to the story's timeline. If that wasn't enough to seal darkness onto the property, the Union soldiers were soon to come, usurp the land right from the Confederates and rightful owners, and eventually torch the house and surrounding farm as the timeline goes.

At this point of the legend, there seems to be a conflict for many of the story elements, adding more confusion to an already complicated history. If the Union soldiers came to take the farm from its Confederate use and set the property ablaze, wouldn't that have burned up many of the slaves underneath the house? Who was left to rise up against when the slave rebellion didn't happen until after the war? The legend, as often reported, even seems to forget a major factor of Southern history in that the very day the Civil War ended (April 9th, 1865); the Emancipation Proclamation was enforced to free all remaining slaves throughout the country. There would not have been slaves there after the abolishment of slavery and certainly not after Union soldiers had been there and ravaged the site as they did, but as there are cemeteries for both slaves and Union soldiers surrounding the property, it's possible that if there was a slave uprising, it would have been between 1860 when Carter died (and not from a slave rebellion) and 1863 when it was used as a Confederate hospital.

Either way, the Moody Brick is said to be bursting at the seams with ghosts and a malevolent atmosphere responsible for unexplained deaths, suicides, and maiming from renovation accidents. Ghosts of slaves and Civil War soldiers have all been reported throughout the site. There is one report of a woman in white who stands at a window holding a candle and looking down at whoever might be looking up at her. She is thought to either be Josephine Moody Sanders or a maid who committed suicide. It is further alleged that the whole Moody Farm is cursed... and that part of the legend, at least, may very well be true.

In 1888, after all the hard work the Moody brothers had put onto the plantation, a fire had broken out across the whole house and property and ruined just about everything for the second time. The conflagration was said to have been caused by a spark from a chimney fire. It was renovated again with a completely different architectural style that made the whole house seem inconsistent and ill-fitting. Later, descendants of the Moody brothers came to possess the house, and tragedy struck Josephine Moody, daughter of John Moody and wife to Pleasant Wyatt Sanders, when their son, Charley B. Sanders, died inside the house in 1913.

Then there is a story of a Joseph Sanders who, seemingly by remarkable coincidence, had his fate slightly entwined with the Moody Brick house before any other member of the Sanders family came onto the property. During the Civil War, he was murdered by his Confederate rebel neighbors after they suspected he was feeding information to the Union. Three men hung Joseph on a mulberry tree and took off by foot with a horse they were using to carry their things. A platoon of Union soldiers apparently got immediate wind of what happened and chased the three men and their horse down to the foot of the mountain, which just happened to be near the site of the Moody Brick. The Union soldiers first killed the horse, made the men dig a grave for it, then killed the men, laid them down into the pit, and rolled their horse on top of them. The three men are now also part of the ghostly horde haunting the property.

A lot of things about The Moody Brick house almost seem too unreal to believe, from the stories themselves to the house itself being fated to live up to its own name, but for all the unpleasantness surrounding the plantation, the local community highly reveres it as a dignified constituent of their Southern culture. Many swear by the ghost lore of the property while others defend it against such nonsense, treasuring its historical value above all else. It's only in the South where you can find people so proud of their heritage that they're willing to find a silver lining in a moody brick.

If that isn't a catchphrase, it should be.

* * * * *

From the very top of the state of Alabama to the very bottom, we travel nearly three-hundred miles south of Jackson County to a small town called Red Level in Covington County. It was named for Read's Level, a store that operated as the designated post office from 1857 to 1866 two miles away before temporarily closing as a result of the Civil War. Red Level was promoted from community to city in 1901 and boasts only a modest few things from its history – it was the home of Surgeon General Luther Terry, who was responsible for cancer warnings being printed on packages of cigarettes during the Kennedy administration, James M. Cassidy, who was the great-great-grandfather of President Bill Clinton, pilot Ben Crum Foshee, who served with the Flying Tigers 1st American Volunteer of the Chinese Air Force between 1941 to

1942, and one of the few churches in the South reputed to be haunted by *banshees*, among a whole slew of other entities said to be stalking every corner of the property.

From one ironically named building to another, our travels bring us to **The Consolation Church of Red Level**. The official name for the building is the Oakey Streak Methodist Church and, like most haunted churches, it has been abandoned for quite some time... for a good reason. There is a wide variety of dark activity surrounding the building, but the rumors seem to focus on there being banshees haunting the church as the reason it is no longer amassing people for worship. As we learned in the *Creatures of the Night* chapter, a banshee is a spirit that appears at night and wails a long, horrible melody almost endlessly from some distance in the darkness. Though rarely seen, the banshee is said to appear as a woman-like figure with a long, dull-colored robe and an aged look resembling one on his or her deathbed. Her cadaverous song is often an ill omen that someone soon is to die, and if anything could presumably clear out a Southern church, it probably would be the idea that the next time you go through those doors will be for your own funeral. The legend doesn't specify who or what the banshees might be, just that the crying and screeching peals could well penetrate through the wooden structure of the building and fill the unfortunate listener with a dread unlike anything they've ever known.

As the story continues, you might consider yourself lucky if the banshee was all you experienced if you just happened to be at the church at night. Outside the building is a cemetery, an outhouse, and gates that either protect the church from vandals or the vandals from the church. On a good night, you might run into a host of Confederate soldier spirits who are marching back and forth on the grounds between the church and gates. On a bad night, you might run into a pack of creatures resembling black dogs with red eyes called "hellhounds." A hellhound is also an omen of death, but one very capable of fulfilling that omen itself by tearing you apart, limb from limb, the first time it gets too close to you.

Among the most terrifying of the harbinger spirits, however, is a pair of children that use the spot as their eternal playground. One is a little boy who appears from thin air and plays with a ball. It is said if he rolls the ball to you, you will soon die. The other child is a little girl who, despite her innocent-looking figure playfully skipping along the road, is hiding a terrifying presence. It is said if you drive by her while she appears alongside the road, she will actually stop your car until she gets ahead of you, and possibly do something unspeakable to you as well.

The outhouse on the property is also said to be rigged by paranormal influence. Should you need to use it for any reason; a poltergeist will close the door once you have gone in and refuse to release the lock until someone from the outside comes to open it for you. According to the legend, the only way one could safely use the outdoor facilities is to awkwardly ask another to join them as they go to use the outhouse, and even then there might not be any guarantee of safety as human possession is also said to occur on occasion around the property, though the folklore does not specify any further on that rather important thing to know.

Finally, it is said if you *really* wear out your welcome at the Oakey Street Methodist Church and none of the other entities are successful at scaring you away, a black, malicious 1964 Ford truck will personally speed down the country road to drive you off the church grounds (and not by giving you a ride).

Most interestingly for a church this haunted, the legend offers not a single clue where all these hyper-vigilant devils might have come from – it's almost as if they just gathered together to scare the living daylights out of anyone who steps foot onto the once-hallowed ground. According to my sources, paranormal investigators have been to the site multiple times and all of them seem to find something confirming their dreadful suspicions.

Should you ever find yourself curious enough to investigate the church for yourself, be forewarned and do not go alone... the last place you want to be when you receive an omen of your impending death is locked in an outhouse.

* * * * *

From Alabama, we travel up to Kentucky for two of the most haunted landmarks you can find in Southern folklore. The first of these is **Mammoth Cave** of Brownsville, Edmonson County in Central Kentucky. Officially known as the Mammoth-Flint Ridge Cave System, it is famous worldwide for being the longest known cave system in the world with over three-hundred-and-ninety miles of passageway, the length of which actually increases almost every year due to new discoveries within the caverns. Outside the tunnels that are made available to visitors is the Mammoth Cave National Park – more than fifty-thousand acres of federally preserved land dedicated in 1941 with tours, camping and a dozen things to see throughout the park. It has been one of the most popular tourist attractions in the South since the 19th century... for both the living and the dead.

The site is said to have amassed more than one-hundred-and-fifty accounts of ghost sightings and has a history almost as long as the cave itself. Some six-thousand years ago, it was first used by several tribes of Native Americans as evidenced by artifacts like gourd fragments, drawings, and even moccasin slippers being found in the Salts Cave section of the system. In 1791, a thirty-one-thousand acre tract of the land was sold by Williard Pollard, and nearly twenty-thousand of those acres were later purchased by a British-American merchant named Thomas Lang, Jr. in 1796. The cave wasn't actually discovered until the following year by either John or Francis Houchin when one of them was hunting and following a wounded bear to the cave's entrance near the Green River (although an alternate account says the Houchin brother was the one who ran into the cave for sanctuary from the angry bear).

Between 1798 and 1812, the cave became significant for its saltpeter reserves, particularly during the War of 1812 when the British blockade on US ports made saltpeter an involuntarily rare commodity (saltpeter is potassium nitrate, a necessarily element for gunpowder). After the war, the property came under new management again and started to grow as a tourist destination until 1839 when it was bought by John Croghan, who briefly turned the cave into a tuberculosis hospital thinking the vapors of the cave could actually cure the disease (which he subsequently died of). Soon after that, Mammoth Cave resumed growth as a tourist attraction. By the 20th century, there were several owners of individual caves within the Mammoth-Flint system, and their competitions for tourist money lead to "The Kentucky Cave Wars," which saw cave owners deliberately trying to sabotage the business of their competitors. The cave and the fifty-thousand acre area surrounding it became National Park land in 1941, and advances in exploration meant that the caverns could finally be detailed and recorded with much greater accuracy. These expeditions through Mammoth Cave continue today.

And, undoubtedly, where you will find a landmark with a long history of human use, you will find spirits. Many people are said to have died within the caves, from the Native Americans who explored the tunnels in Southern prehistory and those who were lost during saltpeter operations, to stranded travelers and those who died of tuberculosis. At least part of Mammoth Cave's fame came from the discovery of mummified remains within the tunnels in the early 19th century. These mummified remains were comprised of the Native Americans who used the caves as a burial place, and others were some of the early European explorers. In 1935, a skeleton some 63" in length was discovered and named "Lost John," as he was speculated to be a man who got lost in the underground maze and starved to death. There is an abundance of sadness in the stale air of the tunnels, and this abundance is said to be the source of many unexplained occurrences permeating the passages.

In general, many visitors claim strange sounds and lights, invisible footsteps, disembodied legs and a female voice that accompanies them on their tours. Some tour guides claim there is a well-dressed ghost wearing a 19th century cummerbund wandering in the darkness, a woman with a knife in her chest starring at passing cars on the highway adjacent to the Mammoth Cave, and a man wearing a striped shirt and suspenders who sometimes joins the tour groups in the tunnels. One tour guide was assaulted by an unseen figure during a tour through the "Methodist Church" portion of the cave in the late 1990s. At that point of the tour, the guide would routinely turn the lights out so that visitors would get to experience what being enveloped in pure darkness is truly like. Suddenly, someone struck the tour guide in the shoulder. Thinking it was the park ranger, who regularly stood by her side during tours, she snapped at him to stop it, but once the lights came back on, she found that there was no one standing to her side, and the park ranger was more than seventy feet away from her.

It is not known who many of these entities in and around the Mammoth Cave are, but other ghosts are not quite as anonymous. One of the better known spirits is said to be the ghost of Floyd Collins, the man who discovered Crystal Cave near Mammoth in 1917. Floyd tried his own hand at making a tourist spot of his property, but did not succeed nearly as well.

He decided to seek greener underground pastures and, in 1925, he came upon the Doyle farm and discovered what came to be known as Sand Cave. With Doyle's permission, Floyd dug out an entrance and began removing stalactites when a rock fell from the ceiling and pinned Floyd to the cavern floor by his leg. When he did not return, his friends and family came looking for him and found him trapped under the rock. As they made efforts to get him out, the press caught on and started reporting it throughout the country. More than twenty-thousand people eventually descended on Sand Cave to observe and help with the operation, but by the time they were finally able to get to Floyd, they found he was already dead.

Two years later, in 1927, Lee Collins, Floyd's father, had signed a rather sleazy deal that not only sold Crystal Cave to enterprising dentist Harry B. Thomas, but also transferred Floyd's body from his previous resting place into a glass coffin to be displayed inside Crystal Cave *as a tourist attraction...* for $10,000. If that wasn't demeaning enough, Floyd's remains were stolen in March of 1929 and later discovered near Green River. For some reason, the thieves took his left leg and just left the rest of him there. To date, the whereabouts of the leg or the thieves has remained unknown, but his ghost is said to provide something of a clue, as he is seen or heard near Crystal Cave calling for someone named "Johnny." He is also said to be an angry trickster, stealing nearby tools and throwing whiskey bottles at people who explore the caves (without any indication as to where he got them).

Another ghost said to be roaming the dark maze of Mammoth Cave in search of someone is a woman named Melissa. In 1843, Melissa lived near the cave and fell in love with her tutor, a Mr. Beverleigh. They began a relationship, but Melissa soon found he was courting another girl on the side and, in her fury and jealousy, decided to make him pay for his infidelity with a strange punishment. She led him down to an area of the cave known as "Purgatory," and then ditched him once he got distracted by the beauty of the tunnels. Her intent was only to leave him down there for just a little while, but after that while and a while longer than that, Melissa became concerned when he didn't show up and went down to retrieve him herself. Although Melissa knew the cavern maze quite well, she was never able to find him. Mr. Beverleigh was never seen again. Fifteen years later, when she was on her deathbed from tuberculosis, she confessed what she did and died soon after. Now her spirit is said to wander eternally in search of the man she may have accidentally murdered so long ago. "Purgatory" indeed.

Finally, it is said that a slave named Stephen Bishop is the most commonly seen ghost on the premises. Stephen was owned by Frank Gorin, who bought Mammoth Cave in 1838, and began operating as one of the most famous tour guides the site had ever had. He actually earned a wage leading people through the tunnels and he hoped one day to earn enough money to buy freedom for him and his wife to travel to Liberia, but this goal was never realized as he died in 1857 of John Croghan's ridiculous scheme to use the vapors of the cave as a cure for tuberculosis. Bishop and Croghan succumbed to the disease soon after, and now it is said that Bishop can still be seen on occasion with his trademark Panama hat, green jacket and striped pants either blowing out candles or even joining the tour groups. Whether Croghan haunts the caves is yet to be seen.

In the years to come, as more discoveries are made within the cave system, we may see more light shed on some of these entities, or we might even come across new ones as excavations sometimes uncover in the realm of ghost lore. Mammoth Cave is an impressive monument to the majesty of the South, and with as much history as it has behind it, very likely there is even more coming up ahead.

* * * * *

In my opinion, there are few other American art forms that truly embody the life and soul of the South more than country music. With just a couple guitars, a fiddle, a mandolin and an upright bass, three minutes of music can pull the whole history and geography of Dixieland back from the past to the present where it still belongs. Country music is one of those rare genres that never seems to age and benefits more by staying stuck in yesterday, keeping to simple forms and singing unpretentious songs about loved ones, the glory of the Lord, and the way things used to be. The music of the South is full of celebration, but even more so tragedy, and the sins and heartbreaks of eras gone by continue to haunt present times because of it.

And at **Bobby Mackey's Music World** in Wilder, Kentucky, this fact takes on a whole new twisted reality with stories of ghosts, poltergeist and demonic activity radiating from the premises as a result of its incredibly dark and disturbing alleged past.

In 1978, Bobby Mackey was an up-and-coming country singer-songwriter from Northern Kentucky who purchased the former Hard Rock Cafe (a restaurant unaffiliated with the Hard Rock Cafe national chain) thinking he would find more success musically and personally owning a popular country nightclub than he would pursuing a recording career in Nashville. He and his wife Janet spent much of their savings converting the old building into Bobby's dream, but over the next few years they began to experience strange occurrences ranging from creepy to downright hostile.

Visions of a multitude of spirits said to have died on the property in decades past have been seen throughout the nightclub. Cold spots are experienced in different parts of the bar, unknown voices call out names of patrons and employees,

106

and even the jukebox is said to occasionally start playing the spirits' favorite songs from the 1930s and 1940s... just to name some of the lighter activities that have made up the legend of Bobby Mackey's Music World.

That legend traces its roots back to 1896, not even one-hundred years before Bobby came to own the building, when the property was said to be a slaughterhouse and the site of one of the most grisly and horrifying murders in Southern history. A young woman named Pearl Bryan, who was the daughter of a wealthy farmer and part of the seemingly aristocratic Greencastle society of Indiana, became pregnant by a suitor named Scott Jackson. Scott Jackson was a student of dentistry and also came from a well-to-do family. Presumably, the idea of there being an illegitimate birth was not something the shared aristocracy of the area was willing to tolerate, so they opted to abort the pregnancy. Pearl and Jackson traveled to Cincinnati to meet up with a friend of Jackson's named Alonzo Walling. The plan was that they would perform the abortion themselves, but Jackson was a far more incompetent medical practitioner than he led on and he tried to perform the abortion with cocaine and *dental instruments*. It was a horrific disaster and now the two men had an injured, screaming woman to deal with. Seeing no way out, they took the maimed Pearl Bryan to a spot in Kentucky near Fort Thomas and murdered her by decapitation.

The legend states that Scott Jackson and Alonzo Walling had ties to a devil-worshipping occult, and it is said the head was removed and dumped in a well as part of a dark ritual to appease Satan. Walling and Jackson were later caught and tried in 1897. They would not reveal the location of Pearl Bryan's head, allegedly fearing punishment from their dark lord, and were sentenced to be executed. In a final act of audacity, just before he was hung, Walling vowed that he would get revenge on his prosecutors for his sentencing, as though he really believed murdering and beheading a pregnant woman after injuring her in an unlicensed abortion procedure was legally justified.

The slaughterhouse that was caught up in the maelstrom of the events was soon abandoned, and it stood empty for many years. In the 1920s, it would see more darkness as a speakeasy and gambling house where it wasn't uncommon for rowdy customers to beat each other to death in drunken brawls. In 1933, a businessman named L.A. "Buck" Brady bought the property and turned it into the "Primrose" tavern and casino. It was a very successful venture that eventually attracted the attention of gangsters from Chicago who wanted in on the business. Buck refused to do business with them and the Primrose suffered their wrath as a result. The feud between Buck and the gangsters eventually exploded when Buck shot gangster Albert "Red" Masterson to death and finally conceded ownership of the casino to them.

More than a decade later, in the 1950s, it became yet another night house of ill-repute called "The Latin Quarter." The Latin Quarter almost made the conflicts of the Primrose seem tame by comparison with even more connections to local gangsters and a seedy owner with a long rap sheet to his name. The owner had a daughter named Johanna who had gotten pregnant by club singer Robert Randall, and he was not happy about it.

Once he learned what had happened, he had Robert murdered through his connections to a local gang. Taking a fatal cue from her murderous father, Johanna responded by poisoning both her father and herself. She later died in the basement of the building at the same place where Pearl Bryan had been murdered... *also* five months pregnant.

Even when the building was the Hard Rock Cafe, malevolence plagued the property as deaths continued to pile up over violent altercations on the premises. It was shut down by police over fatal shootings in 1978 and then soon purchased by Bobby Mackey, who would go on to finally bring some good to the accursed spot in Kentucky.

But if any building in the South deserves to be haunted, it's Bobby Mackey's Music World, and that relatively short history of horror soon caught up to the current staff with a vengeance. Aside from the general collection of activities that continue to be reported, there have been paranormal encounters of much greater detail recounted by staff and customers alike. Nearly all the named figures that died as a result of their business with the building have been seen.

Johanna, for example, is one of the more famous entities haunting the bar. Janet Mackey herself once reported encountering Johanna late one night while she was cleaning the bar after closing. Janet suddenly found that a pale woman was standing in front of her. When asked what she was doing there, the girl said she was waiting for her boyfriend, a man named Robert Randall. She then went on to say, while giggling no less, that her father had murdered Robert, and then she killed him and herself in return. Thoroughly creeped out, Janet left to call the police, but then turned around to find the girl had vanished. As the doors were already locked, and the nightclub already checked for customers, there was no way a living girl could have gotten in.

That was very far from the worst experience Janet had with Johanna at Bobby Mackey's. She also reported a very harrowing story that she and one of their employees, a handyman named Carl Lawson, had in the basement where Pearl and Johanna had died. They heard someone moaning from the basement and both went downstairs to investigate. While Carl went to see who was down there, lead pipe in hand, Janet was filling up a bucket at a nearby sink. Suddenly, a smell of rose-scented perfume, Johanna's favorite, filled the air, the water running into the bucket turned into a black ooze, and then Janet felt someone grab her around the waist and squeeze her violently. Janet fought back and was able to escape and make her way up the stairs. Carl heard the commotion and came after her, but once she got to the top of the stairs, the entity seized her again and threw her back down. What made this encounter particularly terrifying is that Janet was five months pregnant when she was attacked, the same length Johanna and Pearl were when they died. Thankfully, Janet and the baby both survived the plunge down the steps.

Carl himself reported a number of his own encounters with the aggressive apparitions haunting Bobby Mackey's. Just like Janet, Carl also came into contact with Johanna, or maybe a spirit that had stolen her perfume, while cleaning the bar after closing for the night. He didn't see her, but he was savvy enough with spirits to know one was in the room with him when he started smelling a rose-scented fragrance in the air. He asked the spirit something to the effect of "What do you want?" and the spirit responded simply, *"Get out!"* and threw ten glasses that had been stacked on top of the bar at him. Not willing to back down so easily, Carl then challenged the spirit to show itself, and then found himself on the floor after the spirit knocked him down. When he looked up, he did not see a young girl standing before him, he saw a tall man with a hangman's noose around his neck. Finding his cue to leave, Carl ran out of the building to his car, catching a glimpse of the specter glowering down at him from the window.

It is possible Johanna had conspired with one of Pearl Bryan's murderers to attack Carl, but even that encounter paled compared to what came later. Having seen and experienced enough paranormal activity to confirm it was not his mind playing tricks on him (but apparently not enough to make him quit his job) he came into work one day with a bottle of holy water that he planned to pour onto the old, sealed-up well in the basement, the same well that Walling and Jackson reportedly hid Pearl Bryan's head in. As Carl made his way through the main ballroom, he heard something thumping behind him. When he turned around, he saw the outline of something tall and demonic staring down at his now-cowering body. Carl could see red eyes, yellow teeth, and hear something in his head shout out "Hail Satan!" The air turned cold and he claimed his will was being drained by this entity. Carl soon found himself floating six feet over the main stage of the ballroom and the bottle of holy water that he brought boiling over. The minute he regained control of his body, he again bolted out the door.

In early August of 1991, Reverend Glenn Coe was called to the site to perform an exorcism in hopes of driving out the demonic forces haunting Bobby Mackey's Music World and Carl Lawson himself. The exorcism was actually recorded on videotape and was supposedly successful for at least a while (I found half an hour of footage online and while I thought it was fascinating, I personally wouldn't vouch for its authenticity). There was another reported exorcism performed in 1994 that was said to have done nothing in relieving the spiritual tension of the property (possibly because it was already exorcized in 1991?) and it is said that the darkness surrounding the nightclub eventually returned. Ghost sightings of Johanna, headless Pearl, Buck, Red and many others are still reported to this day.

So what does Bobby Mackey himself think of all this supernatural gossip? Surprisingly, Bobby has tried to maintain a healthy skepticism and ignorance of the events reported at his famous bar. His mindset early on was for people to not talk about ghosts and demons haunting his property, thinking it would scare business away when, in fact, it has only increased it into the landmark it is today. In yet another example of Southern ghost lore irony, one could say Bobby's plan to achieve musical recognition outside the mainstream route only truly succeeded thanks to a legend he didn't believe in the first place. Country music has always thrived on stories and tall tales from the past, why would it be any different here?

Although he was not alone in his skepticism, as several investigations have failed to factually link the building to the murder of Pearl Bryan or substantiate the events surrounding Johanna or the other killings alleged to have happened on the property, and even modern paranormal investigation teams have produced mixed results in their findings, with the fact that his website proudly advertises itself as the most haunted nightclub in the U.S., and now even has a sign at its entrance warning customers that they may experience supernatural activity, Bobby appears to have softened his view on the supernatural activities that everyone else around him reports.

His biggest hit, after all, is a song named "Johanna."

Legends of the Cherokee

The world, in the beginning, was an island floating in a sea of water beneath a sky of solid stone. It is held aloft by cords connecting the world to the sky, and when the world gets too old, the cords will break and water will again claim the land. The ground which formed the basis of the Earth came from **Dâyuni'sï**, a water-beetle known to the other animals as "Beaver's grandchild," after it submerged itself deep into the ocean to see what was beneath the darkness of the waters. It dug up the soft mud at the bottom and the dirt floated up and formed a mass above the waters. The animals, who were living in the sky realm known as **Gälûñ'lätï**, wanted to find new land to call home, and sent **Great Buzzard**, the father of all buzzards, to see if the new mass was dry enough to settle. He flew across the entire new world, but became tired by the time he flew over what is now Cherokee land. He flapped his mighty wings against the soft mud with such force that it created the mountains and valleys of the Southern United States as we know them today.

These are just a few of the many colorful legends and stories that make up the mythology of the Cherokee Native Americans. One of the more famous archives of Cherokee folklore, *Myths of the Cherokee* by James Mooney, details this story of creation and more than a hundred other legends explaining how the turkey got its beard, how fish and frogs came to be, how the possum's tale came to be bare, even how the teeth of a deer came to be blunt-shaped. Everything that was elemental in the day-to-day lives of the Cherokee nations has a fascinating tale behind it, full of animals that could talk, think, and sin just like man could, plants with mystic origins, and even their impressions of the white man when first he started to settle in the South.

The stories were passed down over countless generations, but unlike the folklores and mindsets of the European settlers coming from across the ocean, their legends were interwoven with their spirituality and it became real to them. Unlike the white man's Southern folklore, which, as we have seen, tended to illustrate aberrations of nature and things to fear, to the Cherokee, this simply was nature at work. The Cherokee relied very much on nature, so a close harmony with all that nature encompassed was essential. A squirrel was no lesser a being than a man or woman as far as they were concerned. If you killed a deer, you paid your respects and thanked its spirit for providing your family with food during the cruel winter. All things, from the warrior to the bobcat to the rock you just tripped over, possessed spirit and therefore were sacred. The Cherokee did not worship this spirit itself, giving that dedication instead to the Great Spirit **Unelanuhi**, the "apportioner of time," a sun goddess who moved the seasons as she flew through the air. The Cherokee could even be called spiritually optimistic as they held no beliefs that there was a concentrated source of evil anywhere in the cosmos, unlike the Satan of Christianity, and even believed in a fairy-like race of immortal beings called the **Nunne'hi**, who were invisible spirits most of the time, resembled humans when they wanted to produce a form, and lived in designated spots long associated with their presence (now what does that sound like?) But unlike our ghosts, these beings were mostly quite helpful, friendly and even enjoyed dancing and music, although, as we will see in this chapter, they had their share of evil spirits and monsters as well.

If the Cherokee could be judged for being excessive dreamers, one only needs to look at the harsh reality of their history for pushing them to dream of better things than what the real world had to offer. Relying on nature for surviving most of what life had to offer was already dangerous enough, but the Cherokee were devastated numerous times as the white settlers came in and established their governments – from the numerous wars they had to fight in to the smallpox epidemic of 1738 that wiped out half of their population and the Trail of Tears in 1838 that saw thousands die of exposure, disease and starvation. They were subject to the same segregation that discriminated African Americans from American society following the Civil War and would not regain their rights as U.S. citizens until the Civil Rights Movement. That they survived such heavy losses for so long an era with their stories and traditions intact is nothing short of miraculous.

I have been fascinated with everything that is the Cherokee nation, past, present and future, since I was young and in this chapter I hope to do my part in keeping some of their folklore alive and circulating as well. As they practically invented Southern ghost lore, let's listen now to *their* tales of ghostly figures and places hiding in the South.

* * * * *

The Cherokee always seemed to live in areas that were surrounded by thresholds to hidden realms. They hardly even had to wander outside their usual hunting grounds before they got lost and came upon a stranger from one of the other "peoples" that would offer to return them to where they came from, or maybe offer them food and lodging at their own villages before sending them back out. Other times, there may have been a battle with a different Native American tribe that would happen to be just close enough to one of these hidden realms that a surprise reinforcement group would arrive to help the Cherokee out when they needed it the most.

One such story was the **Battle of Nïkwäsï'**, which was a sacred mound located on the Little Tennessee River in what is now Franklin, North Carolina. The Nïkwäsï' was a major center for the Cherokee of the area, as they built a townhouse used for meetings, councils and religious ceremonies at the top of the mound and kept a sacred flame burning at all times in there. The story goes that an unknown tribe from somewhere further southeast were moving their way up through Nïkwäsï', killing and destroying everything in their path for no known reason, until they came to conquer the Cherokee on the mound. The warriors of Nïkwäsï' fought long and hard but just could not overcome this vicious tribe.

As they begun to retreat, a stranger appeared on the Cherokee side of the battlefield, staring down the enemy, and he called for the Nïkwäsï' chief to call off his men as he was going to finish off the enemy with *his* reinforcements. At first, the Nïkwäsï' warriors thought he was a chief from nearby Overhill who brought his own men to drive off the invaders, but they watched instead as hundreds of warriors poured out from the sides of the mound and rushed to the battlefield, ready for blood and war. Even stranger than that, the warriors suddenly became invisible the moment they were outside the settlement, but their weapons and arrows stung and slashed all the same. The invaders had no idea what was going on, but the Nïkwäsï' tribe soon realized they were being helped by the Nunne'hi, who were long said to have lived under the mound itself.

The Nunne'hi made short work of the invaders, and the few remaining survivors fled to the head of Tuckasegee many miles away. The Nunne'hi followed, and the desperate warriors begged to be spared. The Nunne'hi chief listened to their pleas and allowed them to escape back to their homes so they could spread the news of their defeat to their respective villages. It was a Native American custom to spare the last few men for this purpose anyway, but it speaks to the benevolence the Nunne'hi were often credited with.

It is said the invisible warrior tribe still exists today inside the Nĭkwäsĭ' mound in Franklin, protecting the sacred area from anyone who wishes to bring violence to a land set aside for peace. It is also said that many years later, during the Civil War, a group of Union federal soldiers were preparing to ambush a platoon of Confederates who were stationed there when they suddenly saw that it was guarded by a much larger number of men than they were prepared to deal with and canceled the attack. It is said that those men were the same Nunne'hi who protected Nĭkwäsĭ' years ago. Interestingly, the story says the protectors did not take the forms of the Cherokee, but instead took the forms of the Confederate soldiers they were protecting.

Does this mean the Nunne'hi are actually shape-shifters (a reasonable assumption since they already have power over visibility itself), or perhaps they just like to keep up with emerging trends?

* * * * *

Not only did the Cherokee seem to live almost intimately with helpful tribes of ghostly warriors, but other races of even more fantastic qualities seemed to be very common in Southern Native American folklore. Another tribe of spirits was known as the **Yûñwï Tsunsdi'**, meaning "little people," and they are said to be a fairy race that lived in the rock ledges of the mountains.

Unlike the Moon-Eyed People of North Carolina, who were essentially human (see *Creatures of the Night*), the Yûñwï

Tsunsdi' were very similar to the Nunne'hi, and, like fairies, they are said to be much smaller than a normal-sized man, barely reaching up to the knee, with long hair that touched the ground, and helpful but occasionally mischievous dispositions. They have a wonderful reputation of helping Cherokee who get lost in the mountains, particularly children, having a work ethic that included helping the Cherokee finish chores and mend broken items as they slept, and enjoying their own drumming and dancing off in distant corners of the hills uninhabited by men.

However, the generosity and zeal of the Yûñwï Tsunsdi' have their temperamental limits and they do not like to be disturbed at their own home by nosy people, nor do they like to have their existence widely confirmed in the world of men. It is said that if you go snooping around intentionally looking to find the Yûñwï Tsunsdi' and tread on their territory, they will cast a spell on you that leave you completely disoriented and barely able to find your way back home. They are willing to help clear out a whole field of crops, saving the men of the Cherokee village quite a bit of time and effort, but if one goes out to watch them do it, he or she will not survive the night. If you find a tool out in the woods and want to take it home, you must acknowledge the Little People and declare your intentions, otherwise you will be pelted with stones the entire length of the journey back. Finally, as they live so close to the Cherokee settlements, they may act as little angels for a long time until someone in the settlement does something that may seem offensive to the Yûñwï Tsunsdi'. After that, they will simply pack up and move, never to be seen in the area again.

One story detailing the fatal effects of encroaching on the Little Peoples' privacy was the story of a hunter who found snow tracks of what looked to be very small children's' footsteps. Thinking no children could be this far out by themselves, he followed them to a cave that turned out to be the home of the local Yûñwï Tsunsdi'. Although he wasn't in any need, and therefore encroaching on their privacy, they shared their hospitality with him and he stayed for a while in their home. When it was time for him to go back, though, they warned him not to tell anyone where he was, or he would soon die. When the hunter arrived home, he was, of course, pressed by his anxious friends to know where he had been the whole time. The hunter held his tongue for a while, but found the story too irresistible to keep to himself. He blabbed the truth and was found dead several days later.

The Yûñwï Tsunsdi' seem to fit the global folklore archetype of a fairy almost to a tee (the story above itself even resembles a lighter one in a progressive rock song called *Keep It Dark* by the band Genesis), and like the fairies of Ireland, England and Scandinavia, they look like happy, sunny, children's play things to unassuming adults, but they are not to be taken lightly. Historically, fairies can be surprisingly dark entities causing any range of terror, from household mischief to abducting children and replacing them with "changelings" (offspring of fairies or trolls). Although the Little People of the Cherokee have not been known to kidnap children, the similarities are strong enough to suggest that the legends of the Yûñwï Tsunsdi' may have been derived from the folklore of the English or Irish settlers and were revised with elements of the Nunne'hi, which the Yûñwï Tsunsdi' are said to be attributed to.

There are other variations of fairies in Cherokee folklore as well, such as the **Yûñwï Amai'yïnë'hï** (water-dwellers) who live in the water and are prayed to by fishermen needing some help getting a good catch for the day. There are two fairies named **Tsäwa'sï** and **Tsäga'sï** who help hunters that pray to them by offering a skill that allows the hunter to sneak up to the deer or prey of their choice without being seen.

119

There is **De'tsätä**, a fairy who was once a human boy that ran into the woods to avoid a "scratching," which is an old Cherokee treatment (for medical *and* sports purposes) where one's arms are scratched with combs made from rattlesnake teeth, flint arrowheads, glass or anything that could puncture the skin and allow a medicine man to apply medicine directly to the arms, and somehow became one of the Little People. He will sometimes hide a hunter's arrow after it had been shot, and can only be retrieved if you call his name and threaten to "scratch" him if he does not return it.

Finally, there is **Atsil'-dihye'gï** (the fire-carrier), whom the Cherokee were afraid of because they did not know if it was genuinely a spirit or a witch in disguise. It carries with it a light when it goes out at night and will sometimes follow people on walking paths. It is rare to see Atsil'-dihye'gï and no one has gone near it enough to see what it truly is.

So if you ever find yourself wandering deep into the heart of the Cherokee woods and find yourself in a presence of a small life form you've never seen before, take a lesson from the Cherokee and treat all that you find in nature with the utmost respect.

Your life may depend on it...

* * * * *

Fairies aren't the only folklore archetypes that find their way into Cherokee mythology – another common type of legend that you can find in almost every country of the world is one of a great fish, lake monster, or some other type of amphibious beast that has resided in an important local water source since before the age of man. Scotland has the poster child of the trope with the **Loch Ness Monster**, aboriginal Australia has the **Bunyip**, China has the shape-shifting **Jiaolong**, the Northern United States has **Champ** of Lake

Champlain in Vermont, and the Southern United States has the **Däkwä** of the Tennessee River of Toco Creek in Monroe County, Tennessee.

Or *had*, rather, as, unlike many of these other cryptids, the Däkwä has been dead for centuries, and the story of how that came to be is one of the more graphic and thrilling versions of the archetype, a perfect illustration of the warrior spirit of the Cherokee.

At an unknown time of Cherokee history, very likely before the settlers arrived from Europe, a canoe of warriors was making its way down the Tennessee River when the monster fish rose up from the depths beneath them and attacked their boat, throwing the entire party into the water. Each warrior, now completely disoriented, fought the waves and each other to get to the nearest shore before it could return and swallow them whole. Luckily, the Däkwä did not surface again, but they did not survive the ambush unscathed – all but one of their warriors made it back safely. The one that didn't was swallowed whole.

The Däkwä, however, was an enormous fish, and there was enough room inside its cavernous stomach that the swallowed warrior was able to escape instant digestion. He was far from safe, though, and once he came to his senses, he knew he had to get out as soon as possible before it swallowed something else and knocked him into the stomach acids. The only way that was going to happen was to cut his way out through the side, but to make matters worse, he found he did not have his knife; he lost it somewhere as the boat overturned.

The warrior searched frantically for anything sharp that he could pick up and use to hack his way out. He soon came across a number of whole mussel shells that had also yet to be digested. With nothing else to work with, the warrior felt for the shell with the sharpest edge to it and immediately started cutting his way out through the stomach lining.

The Däkwä thrashed about in the waters as its stomach came under attack, and the quaking innards threw the warrior up and down the organ. The acids and scorching body juices that the warrior was lucky to avoid at first were now flying all around him and they burned his flesh almost down to the bones. Both of them were suffering searing amounts of pain, but the warrior refused to give up. He cut, and cut, and cut until finally there was a hole large enough for him to climb out.

The cold water of the river relieved his scalded skin and he pushed through as hard and as fast as he could until he could see the sky above him. Once he broke through the surface, he swam towards his comrades on the shore. When he was able to stand on solid ground, he turned to the Däkwä and watched it die from its wounds, an impressive victory of man over nature if there ever was one.

But as the warrior turned back to the others, he found they were staring at him and muttering things amongst themselves. He asked to know what they were staring at (aside from a man who just *cut his way out of a monster fish*, that is) and one of the warriors directed his attention back to the water's edge where he could see his reflection.

Instead of the young, dark-skinned man he was used to seeing in the water, there was an elderly man with bleached white hair and skin looking back. The stomach acids of the Däkwä had permanently scorched the color right off his body (or, in some versions, the hair as well, leaving him bald for the rest of his days).

Another version of the story is told by Wahnenauhi, a famous Cherokee storyteller from the 1800s, and was also collected into James Mooney's *Myths of the Cherokee*. In this version, a little Cherokee boy was sent to do an errand by his father, but instead of obeying his father, the boy ran down to the river (presumably the same Tennessee River) to goof off. As he played in the sand with a mussel shell that he found on the shore, some of his friends from the village floated by on the river in a canoe and invited him to join. The moment he stepped onto the boat, however, his weight caused it to tip over and send him plunging into the cold waters below.

As he was submerged in the dark river, a giant fish spotted him and swallowed him right then and there. Luckily, the boy landed in a safe spot of the fish's stomach where he would not be digested. After a while, the boy became very hungry and began to look around inside for food he could eat before the fish got a chance to dissolve it. When he couldn't find any, he saw the fish's liver hanging down from up high and, thinking it was dried meat as he was accustomed to back in the village, he took the mussel shell that he was playing with earlier and cut it down. The fish, suddenly overcome with pain and nausea, immediately vomited the boy back up.

There is even an identical tale from the Ojibwe/Chippewa tribes of the United States and Canada where **Manabozho**, the hero of the Anishinaabe (which encompass the Ojibwe) is the warrior who gets stuck inside the monster fish and has to fight to escape. It is an extremely common type of story throughout history that almost every culture can identify with and thus adapt. With water being one of the most essential and dangerous elements of early civilizations across the world, it becomes very understandable that it would be the setting for all kinds of monsters, heroes, gods and spirits that could fill the gaps of understanding. Stories like this taught early man to be careful and watch what he was doing as he paddled down the rapids with food supplies for his family or village.

Of course, just because stories of monsters may carry similarities across nations does not mean they're not true – that's what the legend of the **Kraken** taught us (see *Creatures of the Night*). Maybe those stories are similar for a reason...

* * * * *

Other animals in Cherokee folklore, even the terrible ones, provide some sort of historical significance to how the world came to be. **Känäne'skï Amai'yëhï**, the water spider, brought fire into the world when the **Ani'-Hyûñ'tïkwälâ'skï** (thunders) created fire and put it at the bottom of a sycamore tree on an island far out into the ocean where the other animals could not get to it. Disease came about after a council of small animals, birds and insects conspired to give mankind something to keep their populations in check while avenging their abuses and fallen brothers. Medicine came from the plants, who at were allies with man at the time, when they overheard the animals' conspiracy and used their bodies to create cures for the diseases. The one tobacco plant in all of creation was reclaimed by the unassuming hummingbird after scores of animals, large and small, were all slain by the **Dagûl`kû** that stole it (the Dagûl`kû are *geese*, mind you).

But by far one of the more terrifying "origin" beasts of Cherokee mythology was the **U'la`gû'**, the great yellow jacket, who is said to be the father of all yellow jackets throughout the world.

The U'la`gû' lived in what is now the Nantahala Gorge on U.S. Highway 19 in Macon and Swain Counties of North Carolina. In the days of the Cherokee, it was known as the "land of middle sun" as daylight only reached the bottom of the gorge during midday. It was this dark and difficult place that the U'la`gû' called its nest and it was the old village of Kanu'ga`lâ'yï (brier place) near the Nantahala River that it called its hunting ground. For an unknown number of years, the U'la`gû' was a horrible fact of life for the Cherokee that lived nearby and they lost many of their loved ones to it. It was especially fond of children and its reign of terror showed no signs of ever stopping on its own.

Of course, the villagers did everything in their power to subdue the beast, but what could they do? The U'la`gû' was said to be as large as a *house* and somehow flew much faster than its body shape and weight should have allowed it to. The only warning they got that the U'la`gû' was nearby was a deafening sound of a wind and thunderstorm nearby without a cloud in the sky, which was small consolation knowing that if they weren't able to hide fast enough, a man, woman or child could be snatched right off the ground at any second, never to be seen again.

Finally, the Cherokee came up with a plan that could lead them to the U'la`gû's nest where they could kill it by smoking it out. The warriors of the village set up baited offerings of meat in the forest tied white strings that could lead the hunting party to the monster's lair. The first offerings were too light and the freak insect just swiped them easily and darted out of view, too fast for even the string to be effective in tracing the path to its nest. The warriors then decided to make the next offering very heavy so it wouldn't be able to fly as fast.

This offering was a whole deer and the "string" had the thickness of a full rope to it, just to be sure they could still see it as it flew off. Sure enough, the U'la`gû' came down to claim it and, indeed, it was too heavy to pick up and fly at full speed. The warriors were able to keep up with the beast and they followed it to a cliff side which hid the gorge.

They found its cave from the heavy gusts of wind that came from its wings stirring the air as it devoured the meal. Once they entered the cave, the warriors likely felt more than a little bit anxious at the sheer size of the wax combs it had made for its lair. Looking for a spot to start the fire, they discovered that the U'la`gû' had multitudes of normal-sized yellow jackets, its offspring, suffocating the environment and making it difficult to even breathe without getting stung to death. The warriors retreated back outside and started the fire from there while directing the smoke to go inside.

Luckily, very luckily, the plan worked, and the smoke killed the U'la`gû', and many of its equally ferocious descendants, once and for all. Those that were not killed, however, flew out into the world to start nests of their own and prolong their race. This is how the yellow jacket came to be as we know them today.

And speaking of today, the legend of the U'la`gû' remains an important chapter in the archives of Cherokee folklore. The Nantahala Gorge also goes by the name of Tsgâgûñ'yï (where the yellow jacket was) and the nest itself is known as A`tahi'ta (where they shouted). Although the Cherokee spent much of their history living in harmony with nature, this victory helped to prove that man could be stronger than nature, and sometimes his needs had to come first.

* * * * *

One might think (or hope) that on the list of things a member of an ancient civilization should be afraid of, something as awful as a fish that can swallow a man *and* his canoe whole, or a 40ft. long yellow jacket with speed that defies physical law, would be what peaks out at the top of the list. If you were born of the Cherokee tribe, however, you still had something even worse to watch out for out in the mountains or the valleys, and it was known as the **U`tlûñ'ta**, the spear-finger demon.

On Whiteside Mountain in the Nantahala National Forest is a formation of rocks known as the "Devil's Courthouse," where the grotesque fiend was said to live as she had for countless generations. She is said to be a witch as well as a demon, with the ability to disguise herself as a grandmotherly Cherokee maiden to entice villagers into eventually becoming her prey. When not disguised, her true form is said to be the most odious abomination nature ever wrought onto the face of the Earth, with a yellowish skin that was actually impenetrable rock, a deeply disturbing body odor that attracted flies from miles around, a mouth full of sharp dagger teeth, and a long awl on her right hand that gave her the legendary name. Besides just being a hideous supernatural product of rock, she also commanded power over rock as well – being able to move, cement, and transform into rocks with next to no effort.

When she transformed into her maiden state, many of those qualities were masked by her sorcery. The skin assumed a normal color and texture and the flies would leave with the odor now extinguished, but her teeth and her awl would still remain for some reason and she had to hide them in a shawl as she hunted for children out in the woods or, if none could be found, approached the villages to find a fat, juicy liver to call dinner. Children were, of course, a favorite for their trusting, gullible nature and many a child gleefully ran to the U`tlûñ'ta when called, thinking they were a grandmother figure from the village. They would lie in the lap of the witch while she dressed their hair and lulled them to a sleep from which they would never wake. The witch would then stab the child once the opportunity presented itself, remove and eat the liver right there on the spot. Most of the time, she did it so quickly and easily that she couldn't get caught if she wanted to.

If she did get caught, all she had to do was run from the pursuing warrior party and transform into a stone on the road which either threw them off her path, or at least made her impervious to their weapons. Sometimes the flies that hovered and covered her would give her away, but a Cherokee could not even touch the foul monster without transferring the over-powering smell onto themselves. Doing so guaranteed that they would spend more than four nights sleeping outside their own house, fighting off the flies that came to feed on the stench.

Suddenly, a giant yellow jacket or mammoth fish seems like a far more inviting danger to co-exist with – at least then you can possibly fight it or be warned that they're coming. What do you do with an insane, conniving, demonic murder machine that can't even be injured by weapons?

That was the question that eventually brought a very desperate council to order among the Cherokee. Something had to be done before this creature killed everyone in the settlements. Men traveled from many other villages to attend as well, because sooner or later the U'tlûñ'ta would become their problem as well and the village would not be able to handle it on their own.

It was finally decided the best way to rid the world of this witch was to trap her in a pit and try to throw *everything* at her. Every spear and arrow they could find was going down into the pit at her and she, hopefully, was not going to come out alive. It was a dubious plan to say the least, because they already knew she was largely invulnerable to their weapons, and they probably couldn't bury her successfully as she already commanded frightening powers over the earth. The Cherokee were out of time, however, and this plan was all they had.

The men dug a deep hole on the path to the village and covered it with brush, the same sort of trap they use for dangerous wildlife when they hunted, and then waited for her to come through. Eventually, the U'tlûñ'ta did show up and fell for the trap as they predicted. Immediately, as she hit the bottom, she turned to stone and cursed the warriors who surrounded her. They pounded away with arrows and spears that would have killed any living thing, but her rock skin was just too hard and she started to climb back out of the hole, swiping at anything that moved as she did so. Now the warriors knew, even as they had their enemy trapped in a hole and surrounded, that *they* were the ones who were in trouble. The

U`tlûñ'ta taunted them, for any second now she would be on their level and they would be on her menu.

And then, just as all hope seemed lost, a tsi-kilili bird (Carolina chickadee) came fluttering down from nowhere, singing to the warriors that it knew the weak spot of the U`tlûñ'ta. It then landed on the spear-finger of the demon chirping "Here! Here! Here!" The warriors then fired their arrows at the claw they feared so much and then, finally, there was a screech of pain from the horrible witch. The blood she stole from so many others came gushing out of her hand until she withered and died once and for all.

From that day forward, the tsi-kilili bird became a welcome friend to the Cherokee, renowned for its bravery and its ability to see the truth through the illusions of evil. Without that little chickadee, who knows what would've become of the Cherokee Nation?

But don't start breathing sighs of relief just yet, because that might not be the end of the story. In Tennessee, along the Nolichucky River, is a rock-cliff known as "The Devil's Looking Glass" that hides **The Demon with the Iron-Finger**, a remarkably similar monster of equally voracious appetite. Could the U`tlûñ'ta have survived and simply relocated, or was she part of a *race* of demonic entities?

Now *you* have something topping your list of things to be afraid of.

* * * * *

Moving on to a lighter story... one of my great lifelong privileges as a citizen of the Smoky Mountains in East Tennessee has been my close proximity to Cherokee, North Carolina, the headquarters of the Eastern Band of Cherokee Tribe. Many of my summer vacations I spent at least one day there, and even now I still make semi-annual daytrips across the Great Smoky Mountain National Park to get there, just because I can.

So you might imagine my surprise when I learned through my research on this chapter that there is a chance I've been driving by the entrance to an enchanted land, centered around a magical lake, in a nature sanctuary hidden from man by the **Great White Bear** for over twenty years – and I didn't know it until now.

The area is known as the mountain of **Kuwâ'hï** (mulberry place) and it rests at the foot of Clingman's Dome just slightly more than halfway from Gatlinburg, TN to Cherokee, NC on U.S. Highway 441 South. Clingman's Dome has been an iconic spot on an already epic roadway for more than seventy years. It is credited with the highest point of the Smoky Mountains National Park at 6,643 ft. in elevation, and is the third highest mountain point in the eastern United States. There is an observation tower where visitors can enjoy, on a clear day, more than one hundred miles of visibility throughout the hills adjoining Tennessee to North Carolina. The area has national historical relevance as Newfound Gap, the entrance to Clingman's Dome, was the famous spot where President Franklin Delano Roosevelt officially dedicated the park in September of 1940. The Cherokee had designated it as a sacred area within their mythology well before these accomplishments, however, and the area itself is fit for a sanctuary as the legend describes it.

Kuwâ'hï is the home of the bears (which are plentiful in the Smokies) according to the Cherokee. It was where the bears would have a blow-out party just before the start of their hibernation season. Their chief was the Great White Bear, who knew of an enchanted lake known as Atagâ'hï where wounded bears could have their aches and ills cured simply by swimming one from side of the lake to the other. The lake itself is said to be teeming with life, filled from the bottom to the surface of the water with fish. How one would know that is a mystery, because the water fowl are said to be so plentiful that there isn't even enough space for all of them to settle in the lake. They instead hover in the air until a space finally opens up on the lake for them.

Now, a lake that can cure all and provide thousands of hunting opportunities would sound like an incredible prospect for any tribe, and the Great White Bear knew this. Besides being difficult to find and even harder to get to, the Great White Bear still thought it too risky for any man to lay eyes on, so he cast a spell to make the lake completely invisible to the Cherokee before they learned of it in the first place. So how did they find out about it? Apparently, the bears of the Smoky Mountains could talk in a human language, only amongst themselves, but every so often a Cherokee hunter would overhear some of their conversations and it is likely they learned of it through eavesdropping.

It is further said that the lake did appear to one Cherokee whose heart sympathized with the woodland animals more than most. He truly did not want to hunt the birds, bears, fish or harm them in any way. He found his way to where the Kuwâ'hï was and fasted for several days at the spot while praying and singing its praises throughout the nights. One morning, he woke up and the scenery that he fasted in was gone, replaced with a wide expanse of purple water and more animals in one place than he had ever seen. He swam the length of the waters and took in its many breathtaking sights, but as the morning sun rose higher, the Atagâ'hï began to fade from his sight. He got out of the water just before his visiting time was up, pleased with the experience, and marked the area with stones should he ever want to return. The Cherokee returned home with quite a story to tell, though he felt in his heart he wanted to honor the privilege he received. He did not tell the others where it was – he didn't want to encourage them to visit it.

But that resolve was tested during a very harsh winter that soon followed. The village was battered by the frozen winds of the storms and game all but disappeared from their hunting grounds. It became critical enough for the Cherokee tribe that they asked him to return to the Kuwâ'hï mountain where the lake was and come back with food. With his own family suffering, he had no choice but to agree. He set out soon after, performed the same fasting and prayers, and again woke up at the shore of Atagâ'hï.

Though with some hesitation, he decided to aim for an animal which would provide the most food for the kill, and he chose one of the many bears who were playing in the lake. He fired and struck the bear in its neck. There was an immediate reaction from all the other animals, which were first frozen with shock and confusion trying to comprehend what just happened. What is a human doing here with that bow? This is not supposed to happen; *this is why the lake was hidden in the first place!*

Their confusion was short-lived and it turned to rage almost as quickly. The other bears and animals charged at the Cherokee that was once a compassionate friend to his woodland neighbors, and now a murderous traitor just like all the other humans. He was shred to pieces. The bear he shot, on the other hand, quickly dove into the water to heal his injury while he had time and survived, but the damage to the already coarse relationship between bear and man had been done. The Great Bear swore from then on that no human would ever see Atagâ'hï again, no matter how pure-hearted or reverent he or she was. Never again.

Although I myself am not foolish enough to drive to Newfound Gap to look for this enchanted lake, as the house I live in now comes just at the cusp of the Great Smoky Mountains National Park in Tennessee, I admit I will sometimes go outside, look toward the trees at my right in the distance, and wonder if I'm looking at the direction of the Atagâ'hï at that moment. I wonder if by now the Great White Bear will have changed his mind to let someone like me in, but always rationalize that if they wouldn't tolerate a reverent Cherokee disciple of nature, they wouldn't tolerate anyone of the modern age either.

* * * * *

If we've learned nothing else about the Cherokee by this point in the chapter, we've learned that they were, and continue to be, fantastic storytellers. They created and distributed some of the best folklore the South has to offer, living in an imaginative world surrounded by helpful spirits, enchanted bodies of water full of things that eat man, beings that feasted on their children and all kinds of things that kept them on their toes in a flexible, unpredictable reality.

And being storytellers as skilled as they are, it comes as no surprise that they also have a story that *combines* all those elements into one legend featuring a bizarre race of spirits known to the Cherokee as **Water Cannibals**.

According to legend, the water cannibals were beings that lived up to their names by hunting man as their chief food source around the rivers and lakes of a village. When dawn approaches, the cannibals go searching through the nearby settlements for anyone who is still asleep, kill them with invisible arrows, drag them back to their own homes, and then, to cover their tracks, leave behind a ghostly "clone" of the recently deceased to act in his or her stead. The clone would do and act as the man or woman typically would in life, to fool the other villagers, for a period of seven days and then start to decompose rapidly until the clone becomes a mummified corpse. Friends and family are led to think their loved one simply got sick and died in a short period of time. It is said that this hunting method was so effective that the water cannibals purely got away with it for many, many years.

Then, one day, a man from the Cherokee town of Tïkwäli'tsï (today known as Tuckasegee in North Carolina), became sick beyond the doctors' ability to heal. They told him he was going to die. His friends left him home alone to die because they feared a witch would come after him and torture him on his deathbed, as witches were said to do (also because, the story states, people just were not that considerate in the older days of Cherokee history), and they were almost right when, one morning, an old woman came to the door of his house. She went to the deathly man and invited him to go to her home where she would make him well again. Even though he was so close to dying that he could barely move, something about her words gave him the strength to get up and he agreed to follow her.

They came to the edge of a nearby body of water and she showed him a road that went under the waves to a world just like his. He followed and they came to a settlement with many houses and people. There were hunters, wives, mothers and children like the ones from his own village, just as the old woman said, but as he walked by a hunting party carrying their prey, he found it wasn't bear or deer that fed them in this world, it was people... some of which he even knew from Tïkwäli'tsï.

Very likely unnerved by the surreal sight, he continued to follow the old woman until they got to her home. She made a bed for him and got him where he was comfortable so he could convalesce. When he became hungry, the old woman read his thoughts and tried to prepare him a meal... from one of the dead men they just brought in from Tïkwäli'tsï. She cut a slice of the fallen hunter and roasted it, but the man became horrified at the prospect of eating one of his fellow men. The old woman sympathized and placed her hands on his stomach to conjure up a meal of the beans and grains he was used to.

After a time, the man is able to fully recover and is set to leave the hospitality of the water cannibal. She tells him he must not tell anyone about them or their village for seven days (possibly for a reason similar to why they leave apparitional clones in the stead of their prey for the same amount of time). Gracious for the hospitality, the man does so. For seven days, he refused to answer any questions to where he was or how he got better, but after the seventh day was up, he told all to anyone who wanted to know.

Thus the legend of the water cannibals was born and spread out across the Cherokee. Exactly why the old woman was so benevolent to something that could have just been an easy meal is not known, nor why he was only required to keep such a secretive race secret for a short period of time. The moral of the story seems to be a more creative way of saying "the early bird gets the worms," but it would seem strange that the Cherokee would create such a whole fictional race of terrors that occasionally help people out just for that means.

It's true that many ancient stories of the Native Americans are full of plot holes or lack strong points to what the stories were supposed to be about, but storytelling isn't always about logic, it's about how you can captivate your audience and make them yearn for a similar world of their own.

After all, if you can make a race of murderous water cannibals likable to audiences for centuries, you're clearly doing something right.

Witches of the Hollars

Southern folklore is rich with witchcraft, and legends of witches run so tightly parallel to legends of ghosts and demons that they're almost inseparable. Hundreds of stories featuring evil spirits that were once witches in their former lives, or conjured by a witch to assist in her evil bidding, abound throughout the darkened glades of the mountains and the sickly outskirts of the cities. Every community in the Bible Belt even today, no matter the size, seems to have at least one reclusive figure that is rumored to dabble in the dark arts, secluded in a run-down cabin miles away from prying eyes. They are to the South what vampires are to Transylvania, Romania.

But it should come as no surprise that witches do not originate from the South – in fact, trying to pinpoint a more exact source for their occupation in history is like trying to find a needle in a warehouse full of hay. Men and women of enchantment were said to exist in a wide variety of forms in nearly every ancient culture of the world – the *medicine man* of the Native American tribes, the *kalku* of the Chile Mapuche Tribe, the *tsukimono-suji* "fox witches" of Japan, and the *sangoma* of the Zulu Africans only name a few. Their roles in regional societies are as old as the societies themselves, and they either functioned as scapegoats for plagues and famines, outcasts for having eccentricities or different trains of thought, or even as essential tribe or village personnel who cleared out

137

the bad spirits of an area and performed exorcisms when someone was ill or ill-tempered. How witches arrived in Appalachia is not a question of what country they all immigrated from, but what traditions and fears those who were already immigrating over brought with them.

Even with the existence of good witches in the world, the word itself carries a permanent notoriety. Whenever we hear the word "witch," the first image to come to mind is a bent crone, old as sin and just as corrupt, robed in black with age-worn features and a dominating goal to use her powers for the destruction of mankind. They are obsessed with darkness, blasphemy and vengeance.

Considering the history of witchcraft throughout the world, can we blame them? Being a witch means inheriting thousands of years of persecution and genocide from religious organizations and the simple town folk who do not understand them. The truth of the matter was that the ancient witch was actually probably only the smartest person of the village, a person gifted with logic, alternative knowledge and creativity almost unheard of in the dark ages of that region. This is especially true in the South, as many stories in Southern folklore feature a young man or woman who sets out to find the local sorceress for her help when all conventional logic (for its time) has failed, no matter how ostracized she is from the community because of her failure to conform with traditional religious values. She may offer a potion, berry or method for the youth to try for a successful diagnosis of the problem with surprising success.

Then you have some stories where witches are far from misunderstood geniuses, they are barely even human anymore as they rise from the grave to continue practicing the devil's magic on anyone who might even look like they're trespassing on land they didn't even know belonged to something else.

These witches are now ghosts themselves, or evil spirits whose contempt for human life withstood even death itself.

In this chapter, we will look at stories that feature both sides of this controversial figure in Southern folklore.

* * * * *

"Be careful what you wish for" is a lesson imparted through many types of fables throughout the world. It tries to teach us that cheating to overcome an obstacle (in this case, using magic to bend nature to your fortune) is never worth the effort, and the payment for doing so outweighs the reward in the end. We see this in stories featuring wish-granting genies, adaptations or variations of the famous W.W. Jacobs short story *The Monkey's Paw*, and, more often than not, witches that an ordinary person has set out to consult for an extraordinary problem. One major reason the witch is often associated with evil intent is that asking one for a favor is akin to making a deal with the devil. She will help you and get the job done, but she chooses the method and will not be held responsible for the outcome. Other times, the witch is actually just a kindly old soul and doesn't need to be anything more than helpful, as we saw with the "conjure woman" in *Creatures of the Night*.

In Fannin County, Georgia, there is a classic example of the former with a story dating back to mid-1940s. **Miss Parry** was the name of the local frump that lived in a paper-thin shack up on the hill. Locals called her that because no one knew her first name and likely didn't have the courage to ask her what it was. No one knew anything about her other than she was exceptionally old and mysterious, and yet it was still said that many came seeking her spells and solutions.

One of them was a woman who lived in Gilmer County by the name of Marge who was the self-proclaimed head of her family. She was a bullish woman, heavily opinionated and given to steamrolling her way through the affairs of the family. She had a niece named Lily who was growing up and came to find the man of her dreams with a local moonshiner named Grady Holmes. Grady was a decent enough man, but his business in unlicensed alcohol did not sit well with Lily's proper, Christian family. Like so many Southern families at the time, they held so high a standard for who their children should marry that they wanted to make sure Lily never saw Grady Holmes again. They came to call on Aunt Marge, and she, in turn, came to call on old Miss Parry.

Both Marge and her sister, Lily's mother Hilda, hiked the road to where Miss Parry was said to be and, sure enough, they were greeted by a strange little woman who looked as frail as the tiny stick house she was living in. Marge and Hilda asked Miss Parry if there was anything she could do to stop Lily from wanting to marry Grady and, turning her attention away from the two busybodies, began mixing some ingredients together in a pot, mumbled something that sounded like a spell, and then told them Grady will not be a problem anymore.

Thinking she must've meant that Lily would no longer be interested in seeing the lowbrow shiner-rat, they went back about their business, only to find out Lily had still gone down to the meeting place they spent most evenings and he had not shown up. The next day, as Marge and Hilda were shopping, they learned in an unceremonious fashion that Grady had died in a car crash – he lost control of his truck as he was carrying a shipment of moonshine and collided head on with a tree. The engine exploded and the intensity of the fire inside was fed by the alcohol in the car until the authorities had to remove a charred corpse from the wreckage. As it happened shortly after Marge and Hilda had left the hillside shack, there was little doubt now that Miss Parry was a genuine black magic witch.

140

The second story comes from Dahlonega of Lumpkin County in North Georgia, a city famous for its roots with the Creek and Cherokee Native Americans and as the site of the first major gold rush in the United States back in 1828. Nowadays, the Dahlonega is better known as the "wine capital of Georgia," and as the site of a strange rock pile that acts as both a historical marker for the forest and the gravesite of a Cherokee princess named **Trahlyta**.

The tragedy of Trahlyta is another story of love gone wrong, and where she is buried now is not far from where she lived in life. Not much seems to be known of her early years, other than she was Cherokee royalty and she was renowned for her ageless beauty. It was said that she consulted with someone legends states was the **Witch of Cedar Mountain**, who guided her to the site of a fountain of youth, now known as Porter Springs, that was blessed by the Great Spirit. The water had the power to temporarily stop the aging process in her body and she needed to drink the water periodically to maintain its power, otherwise she would grow old and die all the same.

She did as she was told and won the affections of the men of the tribe, and none more so than a warrior named Wahsega who eventually asked for her hand in marriage. Trahlyta rejected his proposal and Wahsega did not take it well – he kidnapped her shortly afterwards and fled Georgia for a land much further away where the tribe could not take her back. Wahsega kept his now trophy wife almost a prisoner, and her beauty and life did not last too long without the powers of the fountain. She wasted away and when she came near to her death, instead of begging to be released, she asked Wahsega for one final wish – to bury her back in her homeland when she died under a pile of stones, so whoever puts another stone on the pile will be granted good fortune. Some legends even tell that she cried tears of gold in her last days, probably as a strange side effect of the water's power latent in her body.

She died not long after making this plea and Wahsega, likely now seeing the error of his ways, went back to Cedar Mountain and buried her where she lies today underneath a stone pile now some six feet in height.

But the story doesn't end there – it was then said that the Witch of Cedar Mountain, who apparently had taken a shine to Trahlyta, was heartbroken over her kidnapping and death and added a curse onto the stone pile so that whoever *removes* a stone does so at the risk of their lives. It is said that there were two attempts, in much later years, by two road construction companies that tried to move the stone pile so they could get work done and, like the story of Miss Parry, both met with vehicular fatality not long after carrying the stones. Now the stones are set to remain where they are today and the site is recognized by the Georgia Historic Commission.

Both stories offer interesting similarities and reversals for the traditional Southern role of the witch, and even if the Witch of Cedar Mountain could be seen as far more good-hearted than most examples, it doesn't escape the fact that what Trahlyta wished for still eventually brought on her sad demise. For those who believe in the power of witchcraft, there has been a constant, age-old warning that you can't play with the forces of nature and expect to go unpunished. We are not normally given these powers for a *reason*, and those who know this reason often find out much too late...

* * * * *

Haunting gravesites seems to be what most witches spend their immortal time doing nowadays. Throughout the Southern states are many cemeteries that all seem to have at least one witch buried with disdain after a local lynching. Also from Fannin County in Georgia, there is said to be several spirits of witches that haunt the **Tiley Bend Church** and one that will collect leaves from the ground to pile up on her makeshift burial plot. In Aiken, South Carolina, there is a cemetery where the ghost of a witch is said to put flowers over the graves of children for some reason. In Rockville, Tennessee is the Dyer Cemetery that is said to be the site where another trio of women were convicted of witchcraft and now fill the graveyard to the brim with spiritual activity – reports of huge balls of light, full-body apparitions, and something that feels like broom straw scratching across a person's face are just a few of the things rumored to go on there.

But the story surrounding the cemetery of **Pilot Knob** is a more complicated affair. This eerie resting ground is located in Marion, West Kentucky, a small, Southern town and large Amish Community in Crittenden County that was named after Revolutionary War figure Francis Marion, where a girl of only five-years-old is interred. It is said in either the late 1800s to the early 1900s (with the earlier date being much more likely), both the little girl and her mother were said to have been burned at stakes under the accusation of practicing witchcraft. From there, there is a sizable gap in the back-story, as it is not known who burned them, the circumstances surrounding their alleged witchcraft, or even what happened to the mothers' remains. All that is known from there is the daughter was then buried in the Pilot Knob cemetery, by herself, in a plot surrounded by a white picket fence and lined with steel and filled with rocks. For what possible reason would a grave for a child need that extra protection? Or is it precaution?

Well, for whatever reason the undertaker went to those lengths, it did not keep the sorrowful soul in her tomb. In fact, only the white picket fence seems to keep her tied to her cenotaph, and inside that little square she is said to return at night and stare at visitors who happen to be in the cemetery at that time. She makes faces at them, entices them to come closer, and apparently if you're bold enough to lie down over the plot, you'll feel as though she is trying to pull you down with her. It is also said that the little girl is actually trying to sap your life force to add to her own questionable aura and become more powerful in her after-death state. Now it's starting to look like the lynch mob who put her down might not have been as crazy as we initially thought they were...

And now the story takes a completely unexpected turn into even darker territory, because the little witch of Pilot Knob is not the only thing haunting the cemetery. There is another evil entity floating around the grounds known only as **The Watcher**, and as interested as it is in also scaring off trespassers and paranormal enthusiasts, The Watcher is actually after the *little girl*. The Watcher is said to be the ghost of a murdered man who, for some reason entirely unconnected to the story of the witches' demise, is trying to steal the eternal soul of the undead child. The Watcher, to date, has not succeeded because the fence is built with a certain pattern that makes it appear like more than a hundred crosses line her plot and the Watcher cannot cross it for that reason alone. Instead, the Watcher is instead trying to entice her out, probably for the same reason the girl entices visitors in, and is waiting for a break in her fence to finally get in and snatch her away.

A legend like this is exceptionally rare in ghost lore – it's not every day you hear of a story where an evil spirit is *itself* stalked by another evil spirit. Whatever bizarre spiritual warfare is going on there continues into the present time, as at least two separate reports of interested parties going up to Pilot Knob share many of the same elements. Both accounts describe the graveyard as unusually clean for an area with no routine maintenance or security guard, both accounts describe a loud crackling sound followed by a voice that says something to effect of "you go there!" and then the feeling of being watched and followed back to your car. One of those parties was the Louisville Kentucky Ghost Hunters Society and even the lead-up to the graveyard was considerably ominous, as several people they met along their drive refused to give them any additional information on the site, saying simply, "Turn around and go back. Do not go up there."

For a story this dark and strange, there probably is no better way to sum the whole thing up. Just do not go up there.

* * * * *

From Kentucky, we head east to Tuckertown, North Carolina, a former mill village along the Tuckertown Dam and the Yadkin River, with a *very* disturbing witch story that makes Pilot Knob pale by comparison.

At some point in the early-to-mid 1900s, there was a strange old woman, now known as **The Witch of Tuckertown,** who came out of nowhere and forcibly started squatting in an abandoned home. She was a vile, antisocial woman who wasn't satisfied just being a miserable wretch by herself, she was a thief to her neighbors, a borderline feral animal to visitors, and an occultist who evidently brought something so horrible into the world, it eventually scared off the entire village. The woman was eccentric, even by witch standards. She dug up odd holes in her yard and went out at night looking for "spies." An oily smoke could often be seen coming out of her house as she was brewing something hideous in an old pot, and that was about the only real activity most people saw of her when she wasn't stealing food from their gardens and smokehouses.

Then one day, two of her neighbors heard an awful groaning coming from the witch's house and went inside to see if she was ok. They found her on her bed in a gross agony for which she couldn't describe and they left to retrieve their husbands and some other villagers who could help. One of the husbands was a man named Hamp Carter and he had to bring his two-year-old baby girl, Malinda, with them because she

145

couldn't be left alone in the house. The screaming and wailing from the witch went on for hours and it started to get dark outside with some strange atmospheric conditions floating around the property. As Hamp and another man waited at the foot of a staircase with Hamp's baby girl, they heard something upstairs that sounded like a heavy object had dropped from a shelf. While the witch's shrieks got louder and more terrifying, this other noise sounded like it was getting heavier and closer to the stairs.

Finally, Hamp went upstairs to see what this thing was and, carrying a lantern, created a circle of light where a **Dark Mass** of unknown *everything* rolled out into the light, contorting its already vague shape and morphing appendages in and out of its void frame. The men saw everything from eyes and mouths to beaks, bear paws, reptilian limbs and even a bat wing appear and disappear in random intervals. It was like it was trying to find a form it could pass itself off to be, but couldn't decide what would work best. The men were stunned at what they saw.

Just then, Malinda got scared and ran off to find her mom. The dark mass somehow was able to get to her and knocked her down, rolled over her, and absorbed her into its abominable form. Hamp went after her, but got caught himself and nearly absorbed. The other villagers tried to stop it, but nothing they hit it with even grazed its notice. They were able to injure it with the burn of a torch, but after that, it had vanished into the woods and they could not find it again that night. Malinda was never seen again.

The witch eventually recovered, but so did her horrid attitude to all living things. The villagers begged her for answers as to what happened that night and she refused to offer the slightest bit of help. She died only a few years later, keeping all secrets of the Dark Mass with her.

The aftermath of that night destroyed the community. Hamp's wife died of her grief and most of everyone else in the village moved away before they came into bad contact with this thing that was on the loose. The Mass was spotted a few times after that, but for years it avoided complete detection. It was said that, once out of the house, it could then shape-shift into anything it came into contact with and disguise itself when it needed to, but that was not a good enough excuse for Hamp, who spent every waking moment of his life since that night devoted to destroying whatever it is however he can.

Then, one day, he found it and just happened to have the one thing he needed to take it out once and for all. He carried two sticks of dynamite with him once he had the Mass cornered, lit them, and tossed them where the beast could absorb them. It did, and seconds later it exploded into a black rain for nearly half a mile all around.

For Hamp Carter, a bittersweet victory was his. He was still without his wife and daughter, but he got the vengeance he lived for... or maybe only for a little while.

More than a year after the Dark Mass was been destroyed, neighbors who were walking by the house of an old widow who had lived by herself for more than twenty years started hearing moans and groans of pain similar the Tuckertown witch many years before. They attracted the villagers' attention and went to try to help her. As the women went to try to help her, they heard something upstairs thumping around loudly until they saw something black-colored bolt out the door.

It was only then did someone remember the widow said she had been bitten by the Dark Mass once before Carter blew it up, and, come to think of it, she had started to act kind of strange and antisocial since then...

* * * * *

147

Not far from that scene, back in the Uwharries in North Carolina, we move on to a (thankfully) much lighter story. This features another Southern folklore oddity – a *warlock*, which, in lay terms, is essentially a male witch. Folks from the Uwharries called him **Old John** and said that the secret to his magic was a ball that he carried with him wherever he went.

Old John's story is said to have started two-*thousand* years ago in ancient Egypt where he lived for a time, receiving the ball from the pharaohs and being trained to use it, until he migrated further down to Africa and stayed there for several centuries. He came to America by hopping aboard a slave ship bound for South Carolina and apparently traveled the American South until he came to call the Uwharries home. It didn't take long for John to establish an odd reputation with the other citizens of the hills, as he didn't go anywhere without that ball, refused to lend it out, could not be seen doing an ounce of work, could sometimes be heard talking to other "invisible" people in odd languages, and generally didn't seem to need anything from food to entertainment or companionship.

But whereas most witches or warlocks or medicine people used this to malignant advantage, Old John was probably the closest thing to a real life angel anyone in the Uwharries had ever met. John had no interest in the dark arts and he was primarily motivated to use his powers for good. Many days he could be seen in his usual, rag-like outfit, hiking away to someone's house to help cure them of an ill or a malady that befell their crops. His ball came with him everywhere he went and for most occasions, all he had to do was rub it and whisper a spell over it for it to take effect. Only the most serious diseases and disasters were beyond the magic ball's grasp, which might suggest those events were fated to happen by the will of the universe, but every other time, Old John acted as patron saint to those to came to know him in the mountains.

All good things, however, must come to an end, and as the Civil War began its upheaval in Southern society, many of Old John's friends had moved away as they no longer had anything to live for in the Uwharries, and what few remained did not believe in his powers. It seemed that with the detriment in faith came the detriment in John's magic ball, and his seeming immortality waned with it. Now he was just another old mountain man counting down his last days on Earth.

Then, one day, a man by the name of Eb Littleton had gone missing, and his relatives went to Old John for help. It was somewhat surprising his family bothered to look for him at all, as Eb had the reputation of being lazy, cruel, drunk and doing nothing for the family he was supposed to be taking care of other than to make them hate his guts. Old John came to the family house and was going to use his ball in the living room to help find Eb. This sudden faith in the two of them was like a jump-start, and John agreed.

John went to the other side of the room and proceeded to roll the ball so it would go out the door and literally find him, but as it reached the door, it stopped, almost like it hesitated, and instead rolled off to the side at the fireplace. This was confusing to all members of the family, so John rolled it again, and this time it arced without hesitation to fireplace again, resting alongside the ashes. John rolled it again and it again it went to the fireplace ashes... and that's when the sickening realization hit everyone in the room – *it found Eb.*

Then Eb's widow rushed forward, grabbed the magic ball, and hurled it across the room where it shattered to pieces.

The widow immediately confessed to murdering her husband with an axe, cut him up into pieces, and burned the pieces in the fireplace. As horrible as Eb had been to the family, his abuse was far eclipsed by their love for him. As the family drug the woman outside for a private lynching, Old John sank to the floor staring at the fragments of what had sustained him for double millennia. The ball provided him food, entertainment, and companionship... now it was truly gone.

Old John met his long-awaited end shortly thereafter. It was said he looked like he had been dead for thousands of years when he was discovered. He was buried along with the pieces of his companion. Some years later it was said that ghostly visions of John would sometimes make their way around the Uwharries. A loud noise or two might make one think Old John must've dropped his ball in the kitchen, and then they think nothing of it. John was a good man in life, what would anyone have to fear from him?

Actually, interestingly enough, there have also been reports of ghosts dressed like Egyptian pharaohs spotted on occasion too. They are said to be looking for the man who stole their ball more than two-thousand years ago...

* * * * *

Stories involving witches can take some very strange and disturbing forms indeed. Despite common threads in folklore and stereotypical portrayals that have lasted throughout the ages, there is no such thing as a "typical" witch. They are purely unpredictable, follow no patterns or standard formats, and the immeasurable power at their fingertips only gives them greater potential to dodge every conventional idea that they're associated with for their strength and protection. Throughout the volumes of Southern folklore, there are many stories of people in the mountains who learned this only when it was too late, and nowhere do we see this more frighteningly illustrated than the legend of the **Bell Witch** from Adams, Tennessee.

In fact, the terrorizing entity at the center of this nightmare is so aberrant and perplexing that it's only known as the Bell "Witch" simply because no one else knows what to call it.

Some refer to her as a living sorceress while others suppose she is more of a poltergeist or a demon. The legend of the Bell Witch is one of the most famous ghost stories, not just in Southern folklore, but throughout the whole of paranormal history, ranking alongside the **Enfield Poltergeist** and the **Exorcism of Roland Doe** (which was the basis for the *The Exorcist*). Like Roland Doe, the reports behind the legend have inspired or have been directly depicted in numerous films like *The Blair Witch Project, An American Haunting,* and *The Bell Witch Haunting*, just to name a few. Even today, the Bell Witch is sometimes discussed in hushed tones around Adams, lest she happen to hear something she doesn't like and recreate the horrors that made her famous in the first place.

That story begins in 1804 when a man named John Bell first moved his family from North Carolina to the Barren Plains of Tennessee (what would later become the town of Adams in Robertson County). Bell was a farmer with a wife, five children, and a large tract of land he was going to start a new prosperous crop with. Over the next ten years, he made good on his goals and occupied a relatively prominent role in local society. He became wealthy, possessed close to one-thousand acres of land, a dozen slaves, a number of fields to plant in, fathered three more children, and became an Elder of the Red River Baptist Church. John was very much an icon of self-made success and it seemed like he could do no wrong as his farming venture grew and grew.

Then, one day, his luck came to a dark fall from which it would never recover from the moment he met a woman named Kate Batts. Kate was the local crone that the townspeople gossiped was a witch and John made the big mistake of trying to sell her one of his slaves. When it came time to pay, Kate accused John of demanding an excessive amount of interest that was accrued through the transaction. Interestingly for a witch, Kate first tried to punish John *legally* and succeeded in getting him convicted of usury (lending money at an unreasonably high rate of interest, which meant that Kate probably could not pay for the slave in one payment) at the Robertson County Circuit Court. After that, she was able to get him excommunicated from the Red River Baptist Church, and *then* placed a witch's curse on him and members of his family that would lead to an epic downfall for the whole Bell clan.

Sometime later, in late 1817, John Bell was inspecting the cornfield in the north part of his estate and casually hunting for any fat game that he might come across when he saw something that looked like a dog in one of the corn rows. Thinking it to be a stray looking to get a bite from his livestock, John shot it with his musket, but once the smoke cleared from his gun, the creature was nowhere to be found. At this same time, two of his children, Betsy and Drewry Bell, were walking through the Bell orchard when they noticed a woman walking alongside them. She too disappeared once they took notice.

Strange incidents, yes, but no one seemed to think much of it until later in the evening when a symphony of bizarre sounds started surrounding the Bell cabin – sounds of animals fighting, scratching and beating on the walls, as well as someone drinking water from their well kept their attention many hours of the night. The sounds continued the next night and the night after that with no source or explanation found... then they started coming *inside* where it sounded like wings were flapping against the ceiling of the house and rats chewing on the bedposts while they slept. Not long after that, the furniture in the house started moving on its own and the children were complaining that something was yanking the quilts off their bed while they were still under them. Time went on and the disturbances increased to where they started hearing voices emanating from the darkness of their property, either whispering or singing hymns.

As whole weeks of these unearthly occurrences manifested without an end in sight, the Bell family was suffering heavily from lack of sleep and security. John refused to call for help as he did not want to make news of this attack public, but this resolve was tested when the paranormal activity started to center on Betsy. It would abuse her without restraint – slapping her face, pulling her hair, dragging her around the room and even choking her within an inch of her life. John's silence was finally broken as he began to suffer from a strange nervous disorder in his jaw muscles which made even the simple act of eating, among other things, painfully difficult. Enough was enough.

John confided in his good friend and neighbor, James Johnson (or Johnston, as there seems to be two different accounts for his name), and he and his wife offered to stay the night in the Bell house. They investigated what the cause could be and prayed for much of the day. When they retired to bed, they became the new center for this entity's wrath. The quilts were torn right from their hands, the noises filled their heads with frightful thoughts, and it beat them the same way that Betsy had been beaten. By the next morning, it became clear to John and James that they were going to need more help.

A few nights later, additional friends came to congregate with James and the Bell family. When they gathered together to come up with a plan of how to deal with this, a voice that sounded like James started to talk, but when his friends turned to look at him, his mouth was closed and his eyes were probably bugging out of their sockets. The voice started to come from everywhere at once and it repeated the same prayers he spoke the first night he stayed over. Once it was done mimicking him, it changed into a woman's tone, the same witchy tone as before except no longer in whispers or mumbles – this one spoke clearly and boldly, and had enough to talk about to lasts for days and days on end.

153

So strong an impact was this development that those same friends started coming back on a nightly basis to hear this entity speak. This was no mere ghost haunting the Bell house, this was a highly intelligent and charismatic force that had maliciously decided to take up residence and soak in the attention. More visitors outside the usual Bell social circle started coming in to witness the entity, from the Reverend and other townspeople to the obnoxiously curious, and no one ever left disappointed.

It was during one line of questioning from Reverend James Gunn that the entity revealed her identity as the "witch of Kate Batts." Although she also claimed to be the spirit of a Native American and an early settler for the area, this claim struck a major chord with everyone in attendance. The witch spirit was pressed to answer why she was terrorizing the family, and she answered that her mission was to make John Bell suffer and then kill him. Once word of this got out, the whole community was suddenly fixated on the "Bell Witch," as they called her, the Bell family and Kate Batts herself (she was still alive, mind you, and still operating as she had been in the community). The neighbors who knew John and Kate were divided. Supporters for John shunned Kate at every opportunity while those who supported the witch thought John got what was coming to him for his alleged misdeeds as a businessman.

Aside from drinking in personal questions and dispensing whatever answer amused her the most, like a paranormal celebrity Q&A, the entity was also fond of gossip. It had access to information from all over the area and no sins were safely hidden away. Visitors learned of the shames of their neighbors and themselves as broadcast by the Bell Witch for all to hear. Many were mortified at what they heard while some likely found a sick voyeuristic pleasure in it. It was similar in many ways to the exorcism of French woman **Nicole Obry** in 1565, where people came from all over to witness public spectacles of her possession by the demon Beelzebub. Under his infernal siege, Nicole would constantly air dark secrets of the visiting hoard and seemed to revel in all the exposure she was getting while tormenting the innocent, young soul for a lengthy period of time.

In addition, the Bell Witch had an incredible knack for theology and, like Beelzebub before her, used it to debate any proud Christian and visiting minister right into the ground. While it seemed like no one was safe from her wrath as either an evil spirit or pretentious academic scholar, it is said that John Bell Jr., the second oldest Bell child, was unimpressed with her prowess and regularly challenged her malignant authority at every opportunity. A man of considerable learning himself, John Jr. had a boldness that actually impressed the Bell Witch, to the point where she verbally granted him respect in public.

In a short time, word spread well beyond the Barren Plains, as evidenced by a visit from none other than General Andrew Jackson himself. It just so happened that John Bell Jr. had served under Jackson at the Battle of New Orleans some years before in 1814 and now Jackson was offering to return help when they needed it most. Unfortunately, the Bell Witch proved too obstinate even for "Stonewall" Jackson, and the spirit literally taunted him and his backup right off the property.

Hundreds of people would come to witness the presence of the Bell Witch over the next three years and none were refused entry. John accommodated anyone who would come to his house, spending much of his fortune in lodging and feeding visitors, and even giving up much of his land for their horses and wagons. It is suggested that this generosity, which apparently was not characteristic of John before, was his way of trying to make up for cheating Kate Batts in the first place, although it's also possible he was just happy to have company keep her busy so she wouldn't be terrorizing the family otherwise.

Three years is a long time to be weathered by this stormy spirit and John's health suffered heavily. People had come to try to exorcise the demon, but to no avail. One of their last hopes resided in a reputable witchdoctor who went by the name of Dr. Mize in Franklin, Kentucky, and John wanted to send for him to try his luck at the Bell Witch. Fearing what happen if the Witch knew about his plan, he sent Drewry and James to fetch the exorcist at a very early morning hour where he thought she would not be up and around. Not long into their journey, however, the Witch appeared to the two as a sick rabbit lying on the road. Drewry had a soft spot for animals and he took the rabbit with them for some time on their journey until it scampered off much later. Later, the spirit appeared in the Bell home as it always did and bragged about discovering their secret plan.

When Drewry, James and Dr. Mize returned, they confirmed the story to their chagrin. Whether or not the Witch knew about the plan seemed to make little difference, however, as the witchdoctor did not live up to his reputation. His spells and potions were so ineffective that the Bell Witch herself was lecturing him on how to do them properly! When finally he gave up, the Witch wanted to show her "appreciation" of being exorcised by a no-talent hack, and before the doctor was even fully seated on his horse, she made the animal bolt right off the farm, leaving him to hang on the reigns for the entire duration of his ride back to Kentucky while she played tricks on him the whole way.

The Bell Witch's own notoriety continued to grow into what it is today. Unlike Dr. Mize, she was no joke, and her formidable presence still had not finished creating the legend that would surround her for almost two centuries. By the fall of 1820, John Bell was losing his battle to the evil spirit. When yet another of her pranks sent his shoes flying off his own feet, he confessed to his son Drewry that his strength was failing and he would soon die.

Just three months after he said that, not even a week before Christmas, John Bell was found unconscious on the floor of their house. A Dr. George Hopson was called in and, with John Jr., went to the medicine cabinet to see what medicines he was supposed to be taking, but they found, to their horror, the medicines he was supposed to be taking were gone and replaced with a different bottle that John Jr. had never seen before. Suddenly, the voice of the Bell Witch appeared and started singing praises, claiming that the bottle was hers and it was definitely *not* medicine. John Jr. took a straw, dipped it into the vile vial, and gave it to the cat. Both men then watched in near disbelief as it immediately went into a highly convulsive state and died right there on the spot. It was poison, and John only survived until the next morning. He died in his bed with the Witch cursing and taunting him as he breathed the last breaths of his body.

The Bell Witch even refused to give John respite at his own funeral. While everyone who attended was weeping and singing psalms of Christian love, the Witch was laughing and singing obscene, perverse songs with the joyous tone of knowing her mortal enemy was now dead by her hands. The Bell survivors, now without the anchor of their family and estate, without the true focus of the Witch's abuse and contempt, became anxious at what she would do next. They expected she might center on Betsy again, or move on to Drewry or the other children instead.

Instead, the Bell Witch did something truly unexpected – nothing.

Indeed, after the funeral was over, she was quiet. Her baneful presence had simply gone away after almost four years of an unprecedented spiritual assault on the Bell family.

157

Perhaps it was true that her entire mission was simply to rid the world of John Bell, but if so, why did she want to drag it out so long? Being evil is a short and convenient answer, but it doesn't paint the whole picture of the Bell Witch.

Although her reputation as one of the most frightening and sinistral life forms to ever stain the Earth is well-known in Southern folklore, less known is that the Bell Witch was not without her benevolences to other members of the family. John's wife Lucy, for example, was on the other end of the receiving spectrum from Kate, and it is said that she used to compliment Lucy's kindness, sing to her in a genuine voice, and even bring her fruit when she was ill. John and Lucy's oldest child, Jesse, was also on relatively good terms with the spirit as the Witch once gave his wife, Martha, a pair of black stockings and requested that Martha be buried with them when she died. It is said that the Witch even went to check on Jesse once while he was away on a business trip in her incorporeal form. Even Betsy, the child Kate senselessly harassed for no reason, received one last visit from the Witch in 1821, a year after her father's death, when she became engaged to a man named Joshua Gardner. The disembodied voice came to her and urged for her not to marry this man. Why the Witch would come back after disappearing to make this strange plea was unknown to Betsy, but she relented, fearing the wrath she was already very familiar with, and broke her engagement that night (another account suggests that the Witch resumed her haunting of Betsy and Joshua until Betsy broke it off). Since the Witch already had dirt on everyone else in the community, it's possible she knew something on Joshua that she was not willing to keep quiet about even to Betsy, but no reason was ever given.

The most potentially benevolent act that the Bell Witch ever bestowed was onto John Jr., the young man who refused to back down to the evil spirit and won her respect as a result, when she gave him what she would not give anyone else – the truth.

When Kate left Betsy, she promised to return in seven years. Seven years came and, in 1828, she visited John Jr. Her presence stayed with him for two weeks, and it is said the duration of her visit was spent in conversation, not malevolence. Afterwards, she bid him farewell and promised to return to the Bell family in 1935 (although she never did). It was known for a while that John Jr. and the Witch had a strangely close relationship connected by the respect she had for him, but the real depth of this wasn't uncovered until John Jr. revealed to his son, a Dr. Joel Thomas Bell, that the Witch had secretly been having private conversations with him while she haunted the house and family. In these conversations, she would give the true answers to the questions presented to her, but although John Jr. did not seem to shed much light what those answers were, he instead claimed that the Witch foretold him future events, including the Monroe Doctrine, the Civil War, World Wars I and II, and his eventual demise in New Orleans in 1862. The Bell Witch was never officially seen again.

So what do we make of this truly bizarre entity? Was it an evil spirit or simply a scorned neighbor with powers no one was prepared to reckon with? Many questions are left unanswered about the Bell Witch despite a number of thorough researches by contemporary authors like Charles Edwin Price and Pat Fitzhugh, and even documents much closer to that era such as *An Authenticated History of the Bell Witch* (1894) by Martin Van Buren Ingram, which was based on the personal diary of Richard Bell (the seventh child of John and Lucy) still leave holes.

One reason for this may be found in the critical research of the legend of the Bell Witch. With so many wanting to know more about the story of the haunting, it became inevitable that the skeptical community would want to investigate too and, between 2008 and 2012, the Bell Witch became the subject of scrutiny by skeptic researchers Brian Dunning of *Skeptoid* and Ben Radford of *Skeptic Magazine*. Brian found that it was extremely unlikely that Andrew Jackson ever visited the Bell house, as his travels between 1816 and 1820 were well-documented and certainly mentioned nothing about a witch. It is also worth noting that the only other known account of the incident before Ingram's book was a single paragraph in *History of Tennessee* by the Goodspeed Brothers in 1886 that was extremely devoid of famous details, including Andrew Jackson and the death of John Bell. There is also no evidence that Richard Bell's diary, supposedly written thirty years after the incident when he would've been six to nine-years-old at the time, truly exists either and anyone who would have had firsthand knowledge of the Witch's presence was already dead by the time Martin Ingram's book came out.

(For what it's worth, I will point out that Brian Dunning, in 2010, two years after his investigation, was indicted by a grand jury under accusations of, ironically enough, *wire fraud*, and is still fighting the charges as of writing. Make of that what you will.)

When combining those points with the holes in the story and its similarities to the Nicole Obry possession of 1565, it presents a considerable obstacle towards the credibility of the legend. It suggests very heavily that Martin fabricated many of the details and without the evidence to back it up, no better reasonable conclusion can be reached. After all, if a being as chatty and out-going as the Bell Witch had no problem proving herself two-hundred years ago, why wouldn't she continue to do so today?

Even if the story held up to evidence, in my mind, the question I really want to know is "whatever happened to Kate Batts?" – not the Bell Witch persona, but the old woman who started it all after she supposedly got a raw deal buying a slave from John Bell. None of my sources seem to mention what became of her after the Bell family haunting, but the reason for that may be that the ghost lore of the Bell Witch *still* doesn't end there.

Some say the Bell Witch still resides in Adams, TN, and watches over the modern community, gathering dirt and waiting to unleash her supernal pestilence on another person or family. It is also said that the spirit of the Witch now resides in a cave simply known as the "Bell Witch Cave," where she found a home after leaving the Bell family for good. The land that the cave is located on was purchased in more recent times by a man named Bill Eden, who claimed a multitude of paranormal experiences as he opened up his property to curious travelers.

Aside from footsteps and the occasional glimpse of a white form that drifted over the ground, Bill recalled incidents where a group would get quite a surprise as they toured the cave. One skeptical girl got slapped so hard that finger marks were left on her face, another girl who led her group suddenly found herself pressed to the ground by a mysterious weight and had to be carried out, and even a United States soldier was held fast by something unseen. When Bill passed away, it was purchased in 1993 by Chris and Walter Kirby, who made improvements to the cave and continued to encounter unexplainable noises, shapes and energies. It is even said that tampering with the cave may revive the wrath of the Witch, and the Kirbys will receive, on a semi-regular basis, packages containing stones that were taken from tourists of the Bell Witch cave. They return them hoping it will also return a state of normalcy to their lives after experiencing nothing but bad luck and bizarre misfortune.

So even if you do not believe in ghosts, spirits, demons or any of that stuff, it's still never a good idea to disrespect a witch. They're smart, unpredictable, and you don't know what they could truly be capable of. A lot of witches are simply misunderstood and decent people, but others didn't get their bad reputations for nothing... and you don't want to find *that* out the hard way.

Miscellaneous Mysteries
of the South

Throughout this book, we've seen a number of stories featuring creatures that squarely fit into one of several categories (and many that don't), plus a number of stories that fit just as well into a major folklore archetype or speak about an intrinsic aspect of Southern culture and heritage. We've looked at some of the rich highs and so many of the unbelievably dark lows of our regional history, covering so much in-between, that I would like to reserve this chapter for a lighter focus on stories that don't necessarily need to be explored quite as deeply. The stories in this chapter do not neatly fit into any of those categories and they don't speak much about the hardships and tragedies of Southern history... they're just *weird*.

Now that we've done our homework on how ghost lore can teach us about humanity, past and present, let's have some fun. We'll start this journey in South Carolina with the legend of a most unusual tunnel dweller...

* * * * *

If you stood in the middle of a college campus anywhere in the South, or the country for that matter, and started slinging rocks in every direction you could until you ran out (don't actually do this), each and every spot that those delinquent stones land on might be rumored to be haunted. For some reason, higher-learning schools of all kinds soak up urban legends and ghostly folklore like sponges, and they haunt the dark corners of academia more persistently than the entities themselves. One possible reason for this is the often tense atmosphere that colleges impose onto students – usually freshly minted adults who now have to learn how to cope with being on their own, saturated with the stress of grades, deadlines and real failure, while their heads still transition from the superstitions of their youth to the logic and reason of the real world. Not only could this be a source for why campuses are surprising hotspots for legends that would be better suited for campfires, but it could also act as a source for the entities themselves. It's a strange dynamic.

In my research for this book, I certainly had a wide variety of college folk legends to choose from just from Tennessee, Georgia, Alabama and the Carolinas alone, but definitely the most interesting "haunt" coming from a Southern school I found had to be the **Third-Eye Man of USC**. USC is the University of South Carolina in Columbia, a rather prestigious school with many academic accomplishments and recognitions under its name. It is renowned for having the largest collection of Ernest Hemingway in the world, and the largest collection of Robert Burns and Scottish literature outside of Scotland itself. According to *U.S. News and World Report*, it has had the highest and third highest ranking Undergraduate and Graduate International Business programs, respectively, in the country for years, as well as the third highest ranking school psychology doctoral program.

With so many good things to say about USC's commitment to practical, real world knowledge, it seems very out of place that it would have rumors of a very unworldly creature hiding in its underbelly, but for more than sixty years, those rumors continue to be spread both on-campus and off.

No one seems to know much about who or what the Third-Eye Man might be – he's not stated to be a ghost or demon, he's too human to be creature and he's not human enough to be an actual man. All anyone seems to know on him are based on a few reports going back to the mid-part of the 20th century from people who have encountered him in the "catacombs," a steam tunnel system running underneath various buildings and parts of the campus (and some say connect to the State House and the Governor's mansion). Use of the catacombs today is exclusive only to USC administration and any unauthorized entry is punished to the full extent of policy, but that may be a blessing compared to what might happen if you run into the ghastly sewer mutant.

The Third-Eye Man was first reported in 1949 when two USC students spotted a strange looking man dressed in all silver opening one of the manholes on campus. Although the campus manholes lead to the steam tunnels, he was first dubbed the **Sewer Man** by a Christopher Nichols, a student who worked on the campus newsletter and one of the two who first claimed to see him. It was subsequently reported in the campus newsletter which led to a short-lived frenzy about the Sewer Man.

The next report came less than six months later in 1950 and put a series of macabre spins on the Sewer Man story. He was next spotted by an officer with the USC Campus Police during his patrol behind the Longstreet Theatre building. When the officer came to the loading docks of the theater, he found a collection of bloodied chicken parts and feathers from two chickens that had just been mutilated there. Thinking it was some horrible student prank, the officer went to his patrol car to report the incident. When he came back, he found a strange man dressed all in silver bent over the mess either gathering it all together or *eating* it. The officer shone his flashlight on the man and he found the stranger had a discolored face with what looked to be a small, third eye in his forehead. Understandably, the officer got spooked and ran back to his patrol car for backup, but when backup arrived, the stranger and most of the evidence of his disturbance were gone.

While no one believed the officer's wild story at the time, his report would solidify the legend of the Third-Eye Man of USC, but it was still far from the most frightening encounter that was reported. As a result of the bizarre legend, the catacombs became a hangout spot for college students in the years following, and it was apparently also popular as a potential hazing ground for fraternity leaders to break in their pledges.

Well, this came to a stop finally one night in the late 1960s when he was spotted again in his most frightening appearance yet. A fraternity had decided to take some of their pledges down to the catacombs, presumably as part of an initiation, and they barely got inside the tunnels when they were surprised by the silver-suited Third-Eye Man. This time he was described as being "crippled" and carrying a lead pipe. He charged at the students and tackled one of the pledges to the ground, but despite suffering minor cuts and bruises, the pledge and everyone else were able to get away relatively safely.

They immediately contacted the authorities, but despite a thorough sweep of the tunnels and the area, the Third-Eye Man was never found. That was his last reported sighting. And as silly as the stories may seem, the university does not seem to see it that way. Entrance into the tunnels is now strictly forbidden with many places sealed off entirely, and administration seems to look down on even discussing the Third-Eye Man. This, however, does not stop many students and locals from sneaking and prying in to go look for him, as several online forums have shown me.

Even though he hasn't been seen since before the Beatles broke up, and it's quite unlikely the school will be changing their football team to the USC Triclops anytime soon, his eerie legacy will likely carry on for many decades to come. Ghost stories and folklore stick around whether it's a simple, back-country community or one of the most respectable halls of academia in the South.

* * * * *

One of my favorite perks of living in the South is that many areas down here are virtually immune from most natural disasters. Unless you're living towards the eastern coasts, you might not need to worry about hurricanes, earthquakes, tidal waves, or tornados much at all. You have a pretty slim chance of getting flooded out of your house and a blizzard might only bring half a foot of snow (which is still very bothersome, but six inches of snow in the South is still better than *thirty-six* inches of snow in the North). The tradeoff is that we will often get very eccentric weather patterns throughout the year with extreme temperature changes in as short as a days' time. It's not that unusual at all to have 72° one day and then 38° with snow flurries the next. When we say, "If you don't like the weather, just wait an hour or two and it'll change," we're only half-joking!

And even then, on rare occasions, something truly amazing that no one could predict will come down from the skies and baffle the earthbound for as long as a century and a half. **The Kentucky Meat Shower of 1876** is one of the more famous accounts of this happening.

Unlike many of the other mysteries presented in this book, the Kentucky Meat Shower is *verified truth*; however, naturally, the details surrounding it are still somewhat controversial. At 2:00PM on March 3rd of 1876, small pieces of a beef-like substance rained over a Kentucky health resort called the "Olympian Springs," near the town of Bath, for about ten minutes. It was described as a thick shower that soaked the ground, trees, fences and what have you in a relatively small area of five-thousands square yards. The meat ranged from small, reddish-pink flakes and strips to a chunk the size of a square envelope. The sky that day was clear.

Reports of this story first appeared in *Scientific American* and *The New York Times* on March 10th, one week later. As one can imagine, it didn't take long to attract a horde of curious people to the site, many of them scientists who took the remaining samples (as livestock and scavengers nearby had consumed much of it during the week) for testing, while others were able to get their hands on some of the specimens and tasted them to see if it was actually food of some kind. A butcher from Mount Sterling cooked a piece and declared it was edible, while others described it as tasting similar to mutton or venison.

From there, the findings and theories trying to make sense of the event only serve to make it more confusing. Leopold Brandeis published an article in the *Sanitarian* that claimed the substance was actually "nostoc," which he went on to say was like a low form of vegetable matter (pretty unlikely, as nostoc is a form of cyanobacteria that looks like dark green gelatinous material or beads, basically nothing like raw meat), while Dr. A. Mead Edwards, then president of the Network Scientific Association, found there was cartilage and muscle tissue in the samples he retrieved. The most disturbing claim came from Dr. Allan McLane who wrote in the *Medical Record* that he identified the material as lung tissue from a horse or a *human infant*.

Suffice to say, a conclusive identification of the material still eludes history and none of the suggested findings explain how they precipitated down from the sky in the first place. The theories that did try to explain it were arguably as preposterous as the event itself. One idea was that the meat never was in the air, it had been on the ground the whole time and simply swelled up in the rain (which fails for two reasons – the first of which being that the surrounding scavengers would have found and eaten the meat before it swelled up in the rain, and the second being the very simple question, "why would anyone, much less a health spa, cover five-thousand square yards of their property in shredded meat?") while another more popular, and slightly more believable, theory was that the material belonged to a flock of buzzards passing by over the spa that had vomited the contents of their stomachs *en masse*, as buzzards are known to do. However, this theory suffers because no buzzards were seen flying over the area that day. If they had been, they would have had to fly at altitudes too high to be visible from the ground, which would not have preserved the meat in the specimens that there found. The theory also would have required there to be an extremely large number of buzzards flying overhead to cover an area of that size. Possible, but very unlikely.

The Kentucky Meat Shower remains a mystery to locals, folklore and science today, but the phenomenon doesn't end there. Just a short time later in December of 1876 was the **Memphis Snake Rain** in Tennessee, where a heavy downpour had produced a surprise infestation of small, dark brown snakes crawling throughout the city. It was suggested that a hurricane had picked up the snakes from wherever they were and simply dropped them in Memphis when the storm died down. To its credit, although no one actually saw snakes fall from the sky, even *Scientific American* had to ask how it was possible because the snakes that overran Memphis were said to be numbered in the *thousands*.

Then, in 1886, South Carolina was hit with not one, but two very strange rains that turned the phenomenon on its head, so to speak. One was a rain of warm stones that pelted the offices of *News and Courier* at three different times of the day, and the other was a downpour of common rainwater, lasting from morning to late at night, that fell on two graves in the Aiken town cemetery... and nothing else. Although these instances aren't nearly as credible as the Kentucky Meat Storm, one starts to see how the South acquired its reputation for crazy weather.

So if you're coming to visit our section of the world anytime soon, even if the weather man is predicting clear skies for the whole week, bring your umbrella and some snake repellent all the same!

* * * * *

You might remember much earlier in the book, we looked at the types of ghosts and spirits that most entities usually categorize under. One of them was the **Doppelganger**, but we hadn't seen much of any doppelgangers throughout this text... until now.

In his book, *More Haunted Tennessee*, Charles Edwin Price relates a story from West Tennessee about an intensely frightening encounter a girl experienced with a doppelganger. He does not mention a specific time or place and I was not able to find any more information on this particular account, but the story goes that, a long time ago, a girl who lived with her German mother was often told of a legend that on midnight of St. Mark's Eve, April 24th of every year, a host of spirits will start filing into active but empty churches, presumably throughout the world. These spirits are not actual ghosts, but the spiritual doubles of the church members that will die the coming year.

Being very curious, the girl wanted to see for herself if the legend was true. When the coming April 24th finally arrived,

170

she snuck out of her house and went to the family church some fifteen minutes walking distance away. The girl didn't dare tell her religious and superstitious mother where she was going, as the mother took the legend quite seriously.

It was nearly midnight when she got to the church and she hid some distance away so as not to be seen. She soon saw something glowing from the church graveyard and taking form. Scared, she ducked further out of sight before she was spotted. As the procession moved forward, she could make out several people she knew – an elderly parishioner who had been battling a destructive disease for several years, a woman so old she couldn't even remember when she was born and, finally, her own mother. Two weeks later, the prophecy held true and her mother died of a stroke.

But the story doesn't end there and history has a nasty habit of repeating itself, for once that girl grew up and had a family of her own, she made the mistake of telling the story to her own daughter. The daughter was much like her mother and snuck out to see if the legend was true with her own eyes the next April 24th that came about. The daughter apparently did not see the same ghostly procession, but beamed pretty proudly about her adventure all the same to her family at the breakfast table the next morning. The mother chastised her daughter for sneaking out, but the daughter was quick to point out that not only had her mom done the exact same thing when she was young, but she was even outside the night before!

And then the coffee cup the mother was holding exploded into sharp fragments as it hit the floor. The mother's eyes widened with fear and she told the daughter that she was in the house all evening... what the daughter saw was, indeed, a doppelganger.

Two weeks later, the mother, like hers before her, was found dead of a seemingly natural function. The official explanation was that she died of a heart attack; others say she died of fright...

* * * * *

This short entry is one from my own hometown, barely more than a mile from my own house, and it's one that, even if I don't personally believe it, I can certainly attest to it.

In Sevier County, Tennessee, at the entrance to the Great Smoky Mountains National Park, is a thickly forested roadway connecting Pigeon Forge with Gatlinburg known as **The Spur**, and one of the landmarks on the Spur is a reasonably long tunnel that only passengers going from Gatlinburg to Pigeon Forge get to drive through. It is well lit most of the time throughout the year and the bright orange glow and heavily reverberating environment is a stark contrast to the brown, grey and green roadway that it cuts through.

And yet, somehow, every so often, it is reported that some people will drive the entire length of the Spur from Gatlinburg to Pigeon Forge and either never drive through the tunnel or remember driving through it. I have been driving and have been driven through that tunnel for a quarter of a century, as of writing, and I can corroborate that, once in a great while, I will get to Pigeon Forge from Gatlinburg and think, "...wait a minute... didn't I go through the tunnel?"

It wasn't until I started researching for this book that I found I was not the only person having this experience. Juanita Baldwin reports in her book, *Smoky Mountain Ghostlore*, that a couple had written to her with the same experience, and that local folklorists have known and talked about the mystery of the tunnel for some time as well. I don't know how I would have missed it.

While I personally lean on the side of rational thinking for this mystery, I must admit it's very hard to miss the tunnel on the Spur. You can't really be daydreaming so heavily that you miss a bright orange, *loud* tunnel that takes half a minute to go through and driving 50MPH on a twisting mountain road near a river and many solid rock walls at the same time. I don't know of any strange history or events surrounding it (except for a stray post on a paranormal forum by a poster claiming to have seen a man cloaked in black on the side of the road), so I have no idea why the tunnel would be causing this effect randomly.

But now that I know others have experienced it, I'll never be able to drive through it the same way ever again...

* * * * *

As if the threat of dead bodies and spirits coming back to haunt you wasn't dreadful enough, according to folklore throughout the world, sometimes even the *coffins* they're buried in will come after you too! In a metaphysical context, it would make plenty of sense that the last bed a human being will ever rest in would start to absorb his or her supernal energies and emotions and become closely linked with the deceased host, and therefore Southern ghost lore is ripe with stories of coffins moving on their own and generally being a nuisance to the living.

In choosing the most interesting coffin story I could find, I found a rather short one coming from a place called **Buck Fry Hollow**. Although the story does not specify where Buck Fry Hollow is or was (and I was not able to find it myself), the source, *Specters and Spirits of the Appalachian Foothills* by James V. Burchill and Linda J. Crider, has most of its stories based around Georgia, so I may presume it originated from Georgia.

The story goes that late one night, while a man named Eddie Baker was walking home from work along the wagon-trail road that led to his house, as he turned a bend, he found a coffin blocking his path. It was floating in mid-air and it was wide open for some reason. While it was true he was tired from a long day at work, he wasn't prepared to discount the encounter as a product of his mind. Eddie was shaken, but instead of panicking, he actually moved closer to it and tried to touch it to see what it was trying to show him. Just before his hand got close enough, the coffin started floating higher to escape his reach. Eddie moved closer and the coffin continued to float until it was impossible for him to grab a hold of.

As it was now well above him, Eddie decided to make a break for it back to the house, but instead of escaping the annoying spirit box, it actually stayed in the air in front of him as he made his way back home. It did nothing else but just remind Eddie it was still there until he finally got home... and then it just disappeared. By then, the man was hysterical as he tried to relate the story to his wife, but nothing ever came of it and Eddie never saw it again.

Maybe the coffin was an omen that he would soon die? The story doesn't indicate that he died a short while later as most premonition tropes usually would. Maybe it was inviting him to get in? If so, why did it float up out of his grasp? Maybe it was trying to take Eddie straight to the void of death itself? If so, why did it disappear? Usually familiars like these haunt the living for a reason, but this one left as mysterious as it disappeared, wanting nothing but his focused attention.

It's a story that doesn't neatly fit into any of the usual ghost lore archetypes and that's what makes it so interesting.

So if you ever find yourself in this Buck Fry Hollow, possibly in Georgia or anywhere in the South where you might least suspect it, be careful where you tread... you might never know when an errant coffin might be waiting around the bend for you to accidentally take your last steps inside it...

* * * * *

By now, in this late point of the book, you probably think you've heard it all. I know I did. What other weird phantom or goblin or dark artifact could possibly be left to uncover in the eerie netherworld of the South? Well, while I wasn't able to find a lot of good sources to help corroborate the authenticity of this legend, the opportunity to close the chapter with a story of a **Vampire Chair** is simply too good to pass up.

You read that correctly. If folklore in this region of the country is to be believed, somewhere in the South is a wooden rocking chair that drains anyone or presumably anything that sits in it. It is said that once the unlucky person unwillingly chooses the cursed chair, they suddenly become seized by an invisible force until something scratches an uncovered arm, leg, or possibly any exposed skin, to the point where blood is drawn and drips down to the floor. Interestingly, the minute the blood touches the floor underneath or around the chair, the victim is suddenly released, though likely still paralyzed with shock and fear.

If that doesn't sound bizarre enough, the legend of how it came to be more than makes up for it.

This story begins in the earliest years of the 19th century in Shell Creek of Carter County, Tennessee. Two brothers, named Eli and Jacob Odom, had moved to the area and begun a very successful chair-making business from their home up in the mountains. At first they made chairs to trade for goods, but the quality of their chairs had struck a chord with the people they were trading with, and soon, people started wanting to trade chairs with cold, hard cash. By the 1840s, they were making a fortune with their highly sought-after furniture being sold in stores and directly to homes, offices and commercial accommodations. Eli and Jacob's reputation for quality craftsmanship came from their commitment to treated woods and making perfectly carved joints. Their commitment paid off, and the popularity of their chairs spread even further, to the point where whole wagonloads of their brand were being shipped out to the richer homes of Chattanooga and beyond.

One customer, who would indirectly make the Odom brand even more famous for an entirely different reason, was an old woman who lived by herself in a small cabin above the Hiwassee River near Charleston, Tennessee, a little more than forty miles away. Like most elderly recluses of the time, this woman was said to be a servant of the devil, and not just as a witch, but as a vampire as well. No other information about her is known (which is odd for a woman accused of being a *vampire*), but what is known is the intensely horrifying way in which she died – yet another tragic product of the ignorance of others.

It is said that, in 1917, a construction crew was widening a road on a river bluff near Oostanaula Creek, outside of Charleston, when they uncovered the petrified body of an old woman who was buried upside down in the road... with a wooden stake through her heart. The woman was murdered and interred according to age-old vampire traditions and superstitions. The stake through the heart is the obvious tool for destroying the vampire. Her burial in the road was to punish the evil creature by making sure she did not rest in peace with traffic and natural elements pounding her makeshift tomb for eons to come, as well as packing the dirt down and making it difficult for a vampire to claw their way back up. Her facing down was designed to be a "clever" deterrent, as the vampire who might wake up six feet underground, thinking they were facing up, would dig in the wrong direction and actually bury themselves down deeper (although this deterrent would certainly be short-lived since the vampire would eventually figure out that the dirt they were digging was not falling around them and they had all the time in the world to get it right. It's amazing what sort of ideas used to pass for *logic* in our history).

And even though the woman's possessions were then simply scavenged off by neighbors and other ilk, including the two coveted chairs she had ordered from Shell Creek, what truly links her vengeance to one of those chairs was that the stake that murdered her was one of the Odom brothers' *perfectly carved joints*. A bottom leg support, to be precise.

Exactly who suffered that curse and how many victims there are is unknown. There doesn't even seem to be any noteworthy experiences supporting the legend, but it is still said that it did not take the residents of Charleston long to figure out that something was wrong with the chair. Legend has it that it was traded far and wide, from one place to another, by an untold number of terrified owners who refused to keep the chair, but couldn't destroy it either for fear of the curse intensifying.

To this day, no one knows whatever became of it. It might be outside a Tennessee hotel, it might be in storage in South Carolina, on a beachfront in North Carolina, in an aristocratic house in Georgia or a courthouse in Alabama. It might even be in my own house.

It might even be in *yours*...

When They Come Looking For You: Crosscreek Apartment #16

As of February 2013, over 45% of the U.S. population believes in ghosts. Somewhere in that 45% is me contributing 70% of a positive belief in things that go bump in the night (or whenever they feel like it) and more than a couple things I've listed in this book. About two years ago it probably would have been a solid 50%, as I had personally never experienced anything I could call "paranormal" in the traditional sense, but coming from a liberal Lutheran church and refusing to let healthy skepticism be the basis for closed-mindedness, I couldn't believe millions and millions of people throughout the whole of history, including pioneers of science, former and current police officers, and even some of the leaders of the free world, could all be wrong about what they have claimed to experience. Two years later, I'm keeping a healthy skepticism, but I'm telling a different story.

When I first drafted this book, I wanted to include a section that talked about my hometowns in Sevier County, Tennessee – the nearly interconnected cities of Pigeon Forge, Gatlinburg and Sevierville that have been my home, in one city or the other, for more than twenty-five years. As my goal for researching and compiling ghostly folklore from the South was to collect some of the most fascinating tall tales and reports the region had to offer, I was sad to see the local legends here just didn't quite match up in terms of quality. We have some of the typical tropes you find in most towns, but their stories are quite short and, apart from being used in tourism advertising, really do not have much impact in our culture down here.

It becomes fairly ironic (and not too humble if I'm to be completely honest) in that context for me to report that one of the wildest ghost stories and most haunted places I know of in Sevier County was my own home in Sevierville – **Apartment #16 of Crosscreek Village**.

I had moved into Crosscreek in the late Spring of 2006 and it was exactly what I was looking for – a reasonably large enough apartment that was neither too good to afford, nor a slum crawling with people you couldn't trust as far as you could throw them. Basics, no frills, but attractive and functional for a decent price. Even if I looked around now, I probably could not have found a better fit for me than that little townhouse was. I lived in that apartment until Spring of 2012.

But no place is perfect and, up until Summer of 2011, there had been a handful of strange occurrences spread out through the five years I had lived there alone. One of the first incidents happened within a month or so of living there when, while I was cooking something in the oven, I smelled something burning. I thought it couldn't have been my food because it wasn't due to come out for another ten or twelve minutes. I go downstairs and a bag of potato chips was burning up on the stovetop from the heat below it. While it had been stored in a cupboard above it, it was still enough of a distance away that it would've been pretty unlikely it got there by itself, particularly as the bag was not resting against the door at the time and not heavy enough to push the door out and fall as it appeared. I remember experiencing a variety of other bizarre smells that could not have come from anything in my apartment, not the least of which was barbecue meat that I could not afford to buy at the time.

I didn't experience too many things downstairs in the kitchen and living room compared to the bedroom I had upstairs. For years, I remembered waking up with my bed shaking beneath me and no machinery in the floorboards that could have been active and strong enough to shake it. I also used to wake up with the feeling the posters in my room were different and switching around at night, and while this could be explainable by simple half-sleep states, I still have to wonder why I would wake up thinking the exact same thing for more than half a decade. I would sometimes also come up and find posters, without obvious tape wear, taken down and put in odd parts of the room.

I would say the creepiest things I remember in that room both involved something I might call a "shadow man," in that, on two separated occasions between a couple years, I saw fragments of something that might have been a man. The first time, I was downstairs and heard something thump upstairs. I go upstairs, turn on the light, and see something dark just barely make it out of sight under my bed. I remember it first looked like the last four inches of a black shoe that disappeared once I turned the light on. I checked under the bed and saw nothing. It is possible it might have been a large mouse or rat, but in six years of living there, pest control was part of the rent money and I never had any rodents I had seen for sure. The second time came a couple years later when I woke up into a sleep paralysis episode and saw, in the smallest corner of my eye I had the strength to see out of, a dark figure hovering over me from the right side. When eventually it did pass, I simply passed it off as the black television next to my nightstand at first... but it wasn't until the next day I remembered I saw it moving.

I may say if there was anything creepier going on around Crosscreek Village, it *was* going on around Crosscreek Village. While, again, I would not say I had a lot of weird neighbors, I remember getting my fair share of creepy people at the door. Among the creepiest was a young man with blazing red hair and a very out-of-place sharp suit that I saw walking around in the parking lot and, surprisingly enough, up to my door. When I answered it, he started asking me about what church I go to. I first thought he was an odd missionary of some kind and I said

I already go to a Lutheran Church. To my continued surprise, he actually wanted to know more. I just happened to have a church information pamphlet available that I got for him to look through. As he flipped through, he asked me a series of inane questions that I became less interested to answer until he finally asked me one I will never forget.

"So what do you guys do differently than Martin Luther?"

Not being an expert on Dr. Luther and wanting to get him off my front step already, I simply gave him, "Well, we're not anti-Semitic like he was."

Then he shoves the brochure back in my hands, smiles dismissively and says, "Oh, *no thank you.*" He quickly turns and I close the door behind him, but when I go to the window, curious to see where he heads to next, I don't see him again. I probably would not have thought much more of it until sometime later when a resident from somewhere else on the complex called my attention as I was coming back from the mailbox. She pointed out to the green hill down and across the little driveway you need to use to get into the complex and asked if I knew who "that man" was, because she thought he was stalking her and her kids in the apartment village. I did not see a man and she didn't seem to see him after she pointed out either. I think there was an SUV at the hillside away from where she was pointing and it's possible he was inside or obscured behind it, but I never saw anyone. I don't know if anything ever came of that, but I still wonder if that was the same guy.

After a while of taking notice to many of the strange things going on around there, I noticed a person I knew through my brothers had moved in across the street. She is/was an atheist and not someone given to things invisible or supernal. On a chance conversation, whatever topic we were on drifted to what it was like living there and I had shared some of the bizarre things that I had experienced. Her response is one I would have never in a hundred years predicted when she said, "Oh yeah, *I hear voices and I get touched and pushed all the time. This place is definitely haunted.*"

I thought that might be the last word on the subject. It's not every day that an atheist confirms your superstitious suspicions, and it was definitely thought-provoking for someone like me who was always highly interested in the subject but could never get close enough to experience it.

Still, there's always an explanation. What actual evidence did I have? Lots of people get sleep paralysis; it's a known medical occurrence. Just because I didn't see the red-haired guy doesn't mean he was invisible or vanished. Is it really that hard to think a mouse just got upstairs, escaped from my vision and then went back out the way it came? Was the girl across the street really agreeing that the complex was haunted when she might just be making pleasant conversation? Reasonable doubt could account for all those. I still hadn't actually experienced anything.

Until the Summer of 2011.

2011 was a very significant year for my life. In spring of 2011, I had married my best friend, miss Ge'ne Kea. We had courted for some time in a long distance relationship, and now finally she was wearing my ring and taking my name as part of hers. Like me, she professed faith in Jesus and interest in the occult. Descending from Japanese, Filipino and Hawaiian ancestry, she came from a highly religious and spiritual melting pot where ghosts, spirits, and exorcists are all part of daily life. Unlike me, she had witnessed and experienced actual entities in her life back in Hawaii, and her background made her extremely sensitive to their movements. To this day, I still don't know the full depth of her experiences, and it might be years before I ever do.

She moved some distance in with me in my little apartment in Sevierville. It was not the way we planned to share a home at first, as I had planned to have owned a proper house by then and the housing market at the time was just not good for first-time owners. We had to make do with the limited space and resources we had until the right house became available for us. The Spring months that followed were the exactly the adjustment period we had expected, but they were further complicated as several members of her extended family in Hawaii all began to get sick or injured and had to be rushed to the hospital, sometimes multiple family members in one drive. It was at the same time as the Tōhoku earthquake and tsunami that hit Japan in 2011 and was expected to have impacts on Hawaii. Although that disaster did not directly affect any of our family there, the stress added onto everything else going on at the time was almost too much to bear.

Then we noticed, as May started to enter June, something wasn't quite right in the atmosphere. Something was making her uncomfortable, which made me uncomfortable. The atmosphere started to grow somewhat tense and, at first, we just thought that was us trying to get used to each other in an apartment that could really only fit one person comfortably, not really two. That same month, we bought a cage and two zebra finch birds (Ge'ne's favorite pets) to help make the atmosphere more pleasing. It was a male and female pair and we hoped that they would mate and start a family, but instead they seemed nervous and agitated, and we could not figure out why.

As we entered June, the atmosphere, combined with the obnoxious heat and sunlight that burned through our apartment windows for fifteen hours a day, was building into a thick miasma of negativity. A job opportunity for Ge'ne had not worked out and it was, at the immediate time, a major setback. More health concerns piled up both in Hawaii and right here for us. We both started experiencing nightmares almost regularly and her energy level and ability to function were becoming seriously limited. We were also noticing that we both kept seeing something moving in the corner of our eyes, as if one of us was walking behind the other, only to find said spouse has been upstairs or on the couch the entire time. I also kept hearing what I thought was her voice calling me from a distance only; again, to find out it wasn't her. Something was also mimicking me to her ears too.

Then, as we were nearing July, Ge'ne started taking to sleeping on the living room couch, as it was cooler downstairs and better for her back at the time. As she sometimes gets up at night, she will keep a small light on so the room isn't completely dark. One day, when I got up and met her downstairs, she told me that, just a few hours before, at about 5:00AM, she woke up and saw something moving in the archway connecting to the kitchen. It was a large black form, moving fluidly, and it was shaped like a dog. She thought a dog somehow got in until she realized it didn't have any eyes, features, or a collar. The dog form was moving and perched itself like it was waiting for its master to serve its dinner.

She armed herself with the nearest weapon available and a flashlight she kept by her side, and approached slowly to meet who or what was in our kitchen. Predictably, when she got a full view of the kitchen, nothing was in there. She then turned on all the downstairs lights to see if it somehow got by her, but nothing. When she returned to the kitchen for a second look, she saw the birds had been awake for a while already. They were barely moving and not making a sound, which is what a finch does when it is *paralyzed* with fear.

I readily admit that, at first, I didn't believe it. Paranormal fans though we are, logic has to come first. Her sleeping pattern had been wildly thrown out of sync for almost a month now, it's much more likely she dreamt it and thought it really happened. This was the moment she started thinking something else was going on in the apartment, and she began comparing it with other experiences she had in Hawaii. Having not experienced anything that I couldn't write off as purely natural, I was not prepared to accept that this early bad patch was something we couldn't get a handle on and fix. All the same, my mind kept drifting back to some of the weird things I remember experiencing before she came to live with me. The nightmares, coincidences and shadows continued unabated. Her energy level was as low as ever and more bad news kept coming from Hawaii. Everything was building to something, but what? What was going on?

But my role as only a skeptical second-hand observer was to be limited. Just before the nightmare part of this was feeling like it was coming to a peak, we got a knock on our door one Friday afternoon, while Ge'ne was still sleeping on the couch, and I opened the door to find *another* strangely dressed young man with short, red hair and a religious bend on my front step. This time, he was dressed like a European soccer player and mumbling something while trying to shove a card in my hand. I thought he was trying to tell me this card fell out of the front of my apartment, but I saw he had a Bible in his other hand filled with similar cards.

When he finally decided to structure his speech into something I could understand, he started by saying, "H-hi there. Umm... I have a... a strange question to ask you." I agreed to try to answer whatever he was trying to spit out. "Ok, uhh... do you guys have the upstairs part of the apartment here, or just the downstairs?" He was right, that was a strange question to ask. I answered that, yes, this was a townhouse and we had both the upstairs and the downstairs. *"Ok-that's-all-I-wanted-to-know-thank-you!"* and then he scampers off not unlike a chipmunk. I did not see him go to any other apartment.

His card only said one thing on it – "Jesus Takes Away Bad Dreams." It was handwritten on an index card. I turned it over to see what church he was trying to get me to join, but there was nothing on the back. What just happened here?

186

And then I froze for a moment... did he say "guys"? How did he know I wasn't living by myself? He couldn't see Ge'ne from where he was at and while it's natural to assume you don't live by yourself in a crowded apartment complex, it's still not usual to direct a question in plural without actually seeing someone else with you. I kept looking at what the card said, and it was just too chilling to believe.

Even more unbelievable? The bad dreams *really did go away*. That was the day that the marathon of nightmares finally ended, and our cycle of sleep got back to something resembling normal... however, this did not mean our own personal nightmare was over, and whatever cast a pall over this apartment did not seem to be pleased at this intervention.

The day I lost my skepticism came one week later, just when the insanely dense darkness of the summer couldn't possibly get any more volatile. We decided we were going to try to indulge in some summer fun to take our minds off all these ridiculous events by going to the municipal swimming pool in Sevierville. To do this, we went to the nearest K-Mart, bought Ge'ne a new swimsuit and planned to go after lunchtime the next day. We went home, I took out the trash, and we relaxed for the evening looking forward to tomorrow.

But when it came time to go, we could not find her new swimsuit. We searched the small apartment and my car for an hour and it was nowhere to be found. Frustration was building again and tensions were about to flare. We retraced our steps, and the only other place I went the night before was to the complex dumpster just a short walk away. Ge'ne didn't go anywhere and I knew that for a fact. She demanded I go check the dumpster and I vehemently refused. How dumb would I need to be to throw out a brand new swimsuit and not know it? If for no other reason than to please her, I went out and walked to the dumpster to check.

And lo and behold, when I opened the sliding door on the right side of the dumpster and the light from outside flooded in, I saw a K-Mart bag at the top of the heap on the other side of the dumpster. I stared at it for a moment, there was no way that could be the swimsuit, but I couldn't look away from it. How could I check it? I couldn't reach over there. I decided to go around to look, and found there was a sliding door on the other side that I'd never seen or used before. I reached inside, pulled out the K-Mart bag, opened it, and made the discovery that changed my life forever.

There it was – the swimsuit we had bought just the night before. I thought I was going to have a heart attack. There was *no way* it could have been there.

When I walked back to the apartment, dragging my jaw across the floor and making sure my eyes didn't actually burst out of my skull, I presented it to her. When I opened the bag again, the tension building for the last four months had finally erupted. We didn't talk to each other for two full days, which was all the more difficult to maintain in a narrow apartment like one that.

That whole time, the event kept running through my mind. How was it possible? Even if I was dumb enough to somehow throw out a whole one-piece swimsuit without knowing it, I would've thrown it away the night before. It couldn't have been at the top of any heap and it certainly would not have been on the other side of the trash bin that I didn't even know had its own door. I thought for a very dark moment maybe she set me up for it, but no, she's just barely over 5ft. tall and she couldn't reach the door on that strange cement incline it was on without losing her balance. Why would she want to set me up for it anyway? What would she gain?

There was no other logical explanation for it. Something else really was haunting us in the apartment. Once I finally accepted it, I tried to piece together the things that I remembered had been stalking us and couldn't find any connection between any of them.

To date, we only have one clue to what it could have been, and it was the straw that broke the camel's back in early August. Things were still tense at the apartment, and one night Ge'ne was drifting off on the couch while I was sitting on the floor watching TV. She told me the story of what happened only the next day because she didn't want me to know at the time it was happening.

When she started dreaming, she was seeing the scenario that was already playing out in real life – her on the couch and me on the floor. Then, from the darkness of the kitchen, a being that looked like a child's shadow came out of the kitchen and started towards me. Ge'ne immediately woke up and found it was just a dream, but when she fell back asleep, the same dream repeated itself, only the shadow child was stronger and came towards me quicker. This happened about six times, and finally, on the sixth dream, the shadow child got me and threw me up against the couch. Ge'ne woke up once more and told me I needed to sleep with her downstairs in the living room. Being as it was late at night anyway, I obliged and we made a bed on the floor.

This time it was my turn to start dreaming of what was going on in real life. I had three dreams myself, but I only remember one where something dark came over me while I slept and I got up to find my teeth were falling out. At first small teeth, but then larger ones with chunks of my mouth attached to it. Finally, my entire jaw collapsed and I woke up terrified. Ge'ne again dreamt of the shadow child coming over me. We were having, essentially, the *same dreams at the same time.*

She told me the story the next day, and she told me that the shadow child was an entity that she had seen once a year since she was thirteen-years-old. The shadow child was after me because Ge'ne was angry with me, and the child was her emotions manifested into something else. Now our theory was that these entities, whatever they were, were becoming attracted to her from throughout the immediate area. They were congregating to our apartment like moths from a quarter mile around to a porch light. Ge'ne was that beacon.

As I said before, this was the last straw. We had to do something, and we turned to our church for help. We were not able to get our pastor out to bless our apartment immediately, but by early September, he was able to come out. We did the blessing in each room and it didn't even take us an hour. We went outside to wave goodbye to him as he left, and when we re-entered the apartment, as clichéd as it sounds, for the first time in months, we felt the darkness was gone. To prove it, immediately upon the pastor leaving, we saw the finch birds, who barely refused to even stand next to each other, mating. They produced a series of eggs and two healthy babies later in October.

It was over. Ge'ne's family had stopped needing to go to the hospital. The coincidences and shadows were gone. The bad luck had changed over to neutral. The church had ended our personal nightmare. Jesus, indeed, took away the bad dream.

I am now at least 70% sure ghosts and entities at least exist somewhere in our world. Even despite all we went through, I still had not seen a full-body apparition of my own, but if nothing else, I gained a whole new appreciation for the stories I've followed most of my life.

But maybe I just need to be patient.

In spring of 2012, we moved out of the apartment into a house of our own in the south part of Pigeon Forge. I already live next to two legends I've listed in this book, and I'm told by my mystical wife that there is indeed something here too... something that lives on a boulder just on the other side of our property. Thankfully, he is not a dark entity, but I'm not yet brave enough to see exactly what it is.

Whether or not you think this long, crazy story with no real proof supporting it really happened, I hope you enjoyed it all the same. I can't make you believe it, but like the famous man once said, "That's my story – and I'm stickin' to it!"

Index

Bibliography

Book Sources

Best Ghost Tales of South Carolina by Terrance Zepke and Julie Rabun

Ghosts and Haunts from the Appalachian Foothills: Stories and Legends by James Burchill, Linda J. Crider, Peggy Kendrick and Marcia Wright Bonner.

Ghosts of the South Carolina Upcountry by Talmadge Johnson

Ghost Stories From The American South by W.K. McNeil

Haunted Etowah Country, Alabama by Mike Goodson

Haunted Highways: Spooky Stories, Strange Happenings, and Supernatural Sightings by Tom Ogden

Haunted Kentucky by Alan Brown

Haunted North Alabama by Jessica Penot

Haunted Tennessee by Charles Edwin Price

Haunted Uwharries by Fred T. Morgan

More Haunted Tennessee by Charles Edwin Price

Myths of the Cherokee by James Mooney

Specters and Spirits of the Appalachians by James Burchill and Linda J. Crider

The Rough Guide to Unexplained Phenomena: Mysteries and Curiosities of Science, Folklore and Superstition (A Rough Guide Special) by John Michelle and Bob Rickard

Weird U.S.: Your Travel Guide to America's Local Legends and Best Kept Secrets by Mark Moran and Mark Sceurman.

Electronic Sources

- http://americanfolklore.net
- http://chaingangelementary.com
- http://dare.wisc.edu
- http://deborahwilson.blogspot.com
- http://dubitoergosum.net
- http://ghostinvestigator.tripod.com
- http://ghoststoriesandhauntedplaces.blogspot.com
- http://hauntedgeorgia.wordpress.com
- http://insiderracingnews.com
- http://keepingupwiththejones-markjones.blogspot.com
- http://mostlyghosts.com
- http://ncmuseumofhistory.org
- http://paranormal.about.com
- http://pennyspurse.com
- http://scaresandhauntsofcharleston.wordpress.com
- http://skeptoid.com
- http://thecollegejuice.com
- http://themoonlitroad.com
- http://townofwhitebluff.com
- http://usnews.nbcnews.com/_news/2011/01/07/5784265-you-think-birds-falling-from-the-sky-is-weird?lite

- http://voices.yahoo.com/haunted-america-ghosts-red-level-alabama-8766001.html?cat=16
- http://voices.yahoo.com/southern-hospitality-top-5-most-haunted-spots-4209213.html
- http://www.batterycarriagehouse.com
- http://www.bellwitch.org
- http://www.bobbymackey.com/
- http://www.castleofspirits.com
- http://www.cherokeegold.net
- http://www.datelinecarolina.org
- http://www.firstpeople.us
- http://www.flickr.com/photos/auvet/6401407273/
- http://www.freewebs.com/pprg/
- http://www.gandbmagazine.com
- http://www.ghostsofamerica.com
- http://www.ghostsofamerica.com
- http://www.hardcoreracefans.com
- http://www.hauntedhovel.com
- http://www.historicghost.com
- http://www.history.com
- http://www.huffingtonpost.com/2013/02/02/real-ghosts-americans-poll_n_2049485.html
- http://www.ibiblio.org/ghosts
- http://www.johnnorrisbrown.com
- http://www.louisvilleghs.com
- http://www.mapuche.info
- http://www.marionkentucky.org
- http://www.native-languages.org
- http://www.northcarolinaghosts.com
- http://www.nps.gov/grsm
- http://www.paranormalspectrum.com
- http://www.prairieghosts.com

- http://www.realhaunts.com
- http://www.sacred-texts.com
- http://www.sc.edu
- http://www.telliquah.com
- http://www.theshadowlands.net
- http://www.tngenweb.org
- http://www.ultimategullah.com
- http://www.umc.org
- http://www.underworldtales.com
- http://www.wbrz.com/news/raining-snakes
- https://autocww2.colorado.edu
- https://eee.uci.edu